AMARTYA SEN

A Biography

Richa Saxena

rajpal

₹ 165

ISBN : 9789350642313

1st Edition : 2014, 2nd Reprint : 2016

AMARTYA SEN (A Biography) by Richa Saxena

Printed at G.H. Prints Pvt. Ltd., Delhi

RAJPAL & SONS

1590, Madarsa Road, Kashmere Gate, Delhi-110006

Phone : 011-23869812, 23865483, Fax : 011-23867791

website : www.rajpalpublishing.com

e-mail : sales@rajpalpublishing.com

www.facebook.com/rajpalandsons

Amartya Sen
A Biography

CONTENTS

There are only two families in the world,
the haves and have-nots

— *Cervantes* —

1

A DEFINING MOMENT

It was a sunny morning in 1943 in Dhaka, a large city in the province of undivided Bengal. A gentle breeze rustled the leaves of a mango tree that stood at the centre of a neighbourhood in the Wari district. In the shade of the tree, some boys were playing with marbles. Other young boys and girls freely ran in and out of each other's homes, for those were the days doors could be left open to let in the breeze.

In one of the houses, a young boy of ten was playing with a football in his front garden. Upstairs, by the window on the first floor, his father sat on a reclining chair, concentrating on a sheaf of papers on his lap. Dressed in a crisply starched white *kurta-pyjama*, Ashutosh Sen occasionally looked away from his papers to glance down at his son, Babloo. To check on him had become second nature. Although their neighbourhood was safe, he found himself increasingly worried about his family. Just a little while ago, he had read the news of some Hindu stores having been set on fire by Muslim rioters. It was most likely in retaliation to the recent murder of some Muslims. For the first time, Ashutosh Sen found himself feeling relieved that most of his neighbours were Hindus. He had never really thought of people in these terms before. The house in which he lived was after all named *Jagat Kutir*, 'World Cottage'.

•

Dhaka was a city whose identity and sense of security would be tested time and again for many decades to come. In just four years, India would gain independence from the British and the Bengal Province would be divided into East and West Bengal. In 1955, East Bengal would become East Pakistan. And, finally, in 1971, it would come to be known as Bangladesh, and Dhaka would be the capital of the new state. But in 1943, the Sen family was unaware of what was to come.

With a shake of his head, Ashutosh dismissed his thoughts of the rising communal violence and smiled indulgently at Babloo who seemed to be hard at work trying to break a neighbour's window with his football.

"Baba... Baba..." Babloo yelled out to his father, panting hard as he kicked his football across the garden. "When will Ma come home?" He crossed the length of the garden in a flash to retrieve the ball and began to bounce it on his toes, flipping it from one foot to the other.

"Soon, I'm sure. She's been gone for over an hour already; how much shopping can she do!" Ashutosh Sen replied.

Babloo laughed. "You know Ma…" he panted, switching the ball to his right foot.

"Hey, you're getting good at that!" Ashutosh exclaimed.

"I've been practising," his son said with a broad smile.

Watching the sun flash off Babloo's hair, Ashutosh turned his attention back to his work with a sigh. He had a pile of student papers to grade for his chemistry class at Dhaka University and he was eager to get them done before lunch.

Outside, Babloo heard the squeak of the front gate open. He hurriedly looked up, thinking it was his mother. The sight that greeted him chilled him to the bone.

Stumbling in through the gate was a man, feebly crying out, "Help… someone please help…." The man had a large gash on his stomach and was bleeding profusely.

Babloo was rooted to the spot. Upstairs in the bedroom, Ashutosh had not heard anything and was focused on his papers, his brow furrowed. Babloo opened his mouth and let out a loud scream, "Baba!"

Ashutosh shot to his feet even before he looked out the window. To his horror, he saw a bleeding man at his gate and Babloo helping him lie down on a small cement seat in the garden.

"Babloo, stay back!" Ashutosh shouted before turning around to race down the stairs. Running out the front door, he saw the man struggling to talk to Babloo. As he drew closer, he realized he knew him— it was Kader Mian, a poor Muslim labourer who often did odd jobs in the area.

"They stabbed me... they got me..." Kader Mian said in a weak voice.

Ashutosh immediately took command of the situation. When he had come out, he had noticed from the corner of his eye Babloo stepping away from the bleeding man. Now he was standing with his back against a tree in the garden, his eyes riveted on the man. He had never seen so much blood before.

"Amartya!" Ashutosh called out. He often addressed his son by his proper name when angry or upset. The formal address snapped the child out of his horror-struck reverie. "Go inside... Amartya, are you listening?"

"Y... yes... yes, Baba."

"Go inside and get Kader Mian a glass of water. And also get the car keys and a few towels. Quick!"

With a weak "Yes..." Amartya turned and ran back into the house. In his shock he had no idea what to do—he could not recall where his mother kept the towels or the glasses. Stuttering and stumbling around the house, he finally found some towels and filled a glass with water and went running out. Ashutosh grabbed the towels and used them to apply pressure to the wound, hoping to stop the bleeding. Amartya meanwhile helped Kader Mian raise his head and take a few sips of water.

Kader Mian was now delirious and kept murmuring under his breath.

"Kader Mian, you need to get to a hospital. Now try to stand, okay?" Ashutosh said, firm but kind.

With some difficulty and plenty of help from Ashutosh and Amartya, Kader Mian was able to stumble out to the car where Ashutosh laid him on the back seat.

As Ashutosh hurried around to the other side to get in the driver's seat, Amartya called out uncertainly to his father, "Baba...?"

Ashutosh stopped and looked at his ten-year-old son whose face was white. His wife Amita was not back from her shopping yet and Amartya could not be left alone. Ashutosh made a snap decision. "Amartya, get in the back seat with Kader Mian." Then, softly he added, "Keep him talking. I don't want him to become unconscious."

Amartya nodded mutely.

The ride to the hospital was not long but it seemed interminable to the young Amartya. Kader, even in his condition, seemed desperate to talk. He kept repeating, "She told me not to come... she told me it was dangerous..."

"Who told you, Kader?" Amartya asked gently.

"My wife..."

"Why?"

"The Hindus... they hate us..."

Ashutosh's face behind the wheel wore a pained expression.

"So why did you come, Kader?" Amartya asked.

"The children were hungry..."

Slightly turning in his seat, Ashutosh asked, "Kader, this is important, listen… did you see who did this?"

"N… no… they came from nowhere… then just disappeared… I didn't come to steal anything… we are honest labourers… she told me it was dangerous but the children… they were so hungry…." Kader Mian's body shook with sobs.

"It's okay…" murmured Amartya, at a loss for words. He had heard his parents talk about riots and murders in Dhaka but suddenly it all became real. People were killing each other because they belonged to a different religion. The man was losing his life because his family didn't have enough food. It made no sense. He wasted so much food on his plate everyday. How could there be people who didn't have anything to eat?

On reaching the hospital, they rushed Kader inside and sat down in the waiting room. Amartya sat ramrod straight, silent, unblinking. The ten-year-old's mind had been deeply affected. Ashutosh too sat in his own silence, his arm protectively wrapped around Amartya. A full half hour went by in total silence, save for the ticking of a clock on the waiting room wall and the distant footsteps of the doctors and nurses attending to patients. Finally a doctor walked out of the ward with a grave look on his face that said it all. Kader Mian could not be saved.

With a sigh, Ashutosh stood up and followed the doctor to make the payments and do the paper work. The police had arrived to get his statement as well. Amartya remained seated. He had not moved. In his mind, he could still hear the dying man's last words, "The children… they were so hungry…"

For many months after, Amartya would recall Kader Mian's face and his helplessness. He often spoke about how unfair it was that the man had died just trying to earn enough to buy some food for his children, that he had died just because he happened to be a Muslim looking for honest work in a Hindu neighbourhood. His parents consoled the distraught child, hoping Amartya would be able to set the incident behind him. Fortunately, a child's mind does not hold on to bad experiences. Their efforts succeeded, and over time Amartya once again became the carefree boy they knew.

But Amartya did not forget Kader Mian. The memory of the man who had died to save his children would return to him time and again. The futility of Kader Mian's death had left a mark on him and, years later, as a student of economics, he would often think about the economic pressures that had cost Kader Mian his life. At the age of ten, Amartya had discovered within himself concern and anger over an issue that he would go on to frequently write about, teach, discuss, and even one day win the Nobel Prize for.

Education is the acquisition of the art of the utilisation of knowledge

— *Alfred North Whitehead* —

2

CHILDHOOD IN SANTINIKETAN

Two years had passed since that day, and Amartya was now far from Dhaka, at the home of his *Nana*, his maternal grandfather, in Santiniketan. A small town in the Birbhum district of Bengal, Santiniketan was famous for Visva-Bharati, a school set up near Bolpur by the revered Bengali poet and Nobel Laureate, Rabindranath Tagore (1861–1941).

Being in Santiniketan was a wonderful new experience for Amartya. Unlike the concrete jungle of Dhaka, this town was surrounded by lush green meadows and red sand. Standing on the terrace, Amartya was awestruck by the blades of grass swaying to the gentle breeze and trees like *sal, palash*, mango and date palms. Looking up, he caught sight of a rainbow arched across the sky and the sun's rays passing through the leaves, making pretty filigree patterns on the ground.

This place was unlike any Amartya had ever seen. Although he had been born in Santiniketan on November 3, 1933, he had been just three years old when his parents had moved to Mandalay where his father taught at the Agricultural College. And he had been six when the family moved from Mandalay to Dhaka for Ashutosh's job as a chemistry professor at Dhaka University. Amartya had been raised in cities, in campuses, and Santiniketan was quite certainly more beautiful than any place he had ever visited. But there was something else about Santiniketan that drew Amartya to it even at that young age. They say a man always returns to the place where he was born. Amartya didn't know at the time that it was to be the first of many returns.

Amartya was aware that the family had come to Santiniketan not just to visit his grandfather, Kshiti Mohan Sen. The town was to be his new home for the duration of his schooling at Visva-Bharati, the school his grandfather had helped Tagore set up, the school where his mother too had studied.

It was Rabindranath Tagore's father, Maehashi Debendra, who had laid the foundations of Santiniketan as an academic town when he first established a small ashram there in 1863. Nearly 40 years later, in 1901, Tagore started a school in Santiniketan named Patha Bhavan that grew from a single class held under a tree to the well-respected Visva-Bharati set up with the financial backing of the Maharaja of Tripura in 1921. The university's Sanskrit motto was '*Yatra visvam bhavati eka-nidam*' (Where the world makes one single nest), a motto Santiniketan truly embraced and continues to do even to this day.

Tagore was truly a Renaissance Man, in equal parts a skilled musician, playwright, poet, artist and essayist. In an article he wrote for the Nobel Prize committee, Sen described Tagore as, "a towering figure in the millennium-old literature of Bengal." Although the West placed much emphasis on the religious and mystical elements in his writing, Tagore was in fact a deeply pragmatic, rational man, with his feet grounded in scientific rationalism. Under his influence, Santiniketan was established as a school that instilled the values of Indian culture and patriotism in every student but also welcomed the modern ideas of the West. The teaching philosophy of the school was based on Tagore's belief that mere bookish knowledge cloisters the mind, preventing independent thought. He also saw Nature as a great teacher and thus established this institution far from the turmoil of human habitation, under the open sky, amidst wild trees, plants and animals.

The school is a residential institution, international in its outlook, but much like an ashram in spirit, still following the principles of the ancient *gurukul* system in which students were taught a wide mix of subjects, both academic and practical. Today, its several schools include China Bhavan (China faculty), Kala Bhavan (college of arts and crafts) and Sangeet Bhavan (school of dance and music). Amartya later said about Santiniketan, "The curriculum of the school did not neglect India's cultural, analytical and scientific heritage, but was very involved also with the rest of the world." Even today, Visva-Bharati is considered one of the finest traditional educational institutions in the country with eminent alumni like filmmaker Satyajit Ray and former prime minister Indira Gandhi.

For Tagore, however, Santiniketan was not just a school but also his home. The poet himself lived on the campus and wrote many of his most famous works there. Said Sen in his essay, "Most of his work was written at Santiniketan, the small town that grew around the school he founded in Bengal in 1901, and he not only conceived there an imaginative and innovative system of education, but through his writings and his influence on students and teachers, he was able to use the school as a base from which he could take a major part in India's social, political, and cultural movements."

•

Looking for her son around the house, Amita Sen found him on the terrace, gazing outside.

"What's the matter, Babloo?"

Smiling, he said, "Oh, nothing, Ma. I was just looking around. This place is so beautiful!"

Smiling back, she said, "That's why it is called Santiniketan, 'the abode of peace'. Do you know, this is where you were born?"

"You mean I wasn't born in Dhaka?" asked a puzzled Babloo whose earliest memories were from there.

"No, you were born right here! We Bengali women always deliver the first child in our parents' home. So I came here a few days before you were born."

"I wish Nana had come back to Dhaka with us. Why

didn't he?"

"Oh, Babloo, my father loves Santiniketan too much. He would never leave it. Do you know he was friends with Rabindranath Tagore who set up this school?

"Really?"

"Oh yes, Tagore even asked him to become the principal of the Santiniketan *brahmacharya* ashram in 1908."

•

Babloo's scholastic influences didn't stop at his father and grandfather. His mother Amita too was a well-known writer and editor of a literary magazine in Bengal called *Shreoshi*. Unlike her son, however, Amita's interests transcended academia into art and culture. Born in 1913 in the Sonarang village of Dhaka, Amita was the youngest daughter of Kshiti Mohan Sen and Kironbala Sen. As a child, she had been deeply influenced by her father's association with Tagore. Raised on *Rabindra Sangeet,* songs written by Rabindranath Tagore, she developed a love for the poet's work and performed many of his dance-dramas, even though at the time it was quite unusual for girls to give public performances. She went on to complete her schooling at Santiniketan and had the fortune of being taught by Tagore himself. Amita even went on to write a book entitled *Santiniketan Asharm Kanya*, after which she came to be known as *Ashram Kanya* (daughter of the hermitage) herself.

Going back a generation, Amartya's grandfather, Kshiti Mohan Sen, too was a prominent figure on the Bengali literary scene and known for being fluent in Sanskrit, Bengali, Hindi,

English, Gujarati, Rajasthani, Arabic and Persian! After completing his post graduation in Sanskrit from Calcutta University in 1902, the title '*Shastri*' was conferred upon him. In 1953, he served as temporary Vice Chancellor of Visva-Bharati and later conducted extensive research on medieval ascetics and the religious sub-community of wandering mendicants in Bangladesh known as Bauls. Sen was well versed in the Hindu scriptures besides having a deep knowledge of music and Ayurveda, the ancient Indian system of medicine. He also authored many books in Bengali including *Kabir* (1910–11), *Bharatiya Madhyayuger Sadhanar Dhara* (1930), *Bharater Sangskrti* (1943) and *Banglar Sadhana* (1945) to name a few and received awards like the Rabindra Memorial Gold Medal, the Deshikottam and the Murarka Prize (1953).

It was no wonder then that Amartya's family unanimously agreed that he must complete his education at Santiniketan. The place, Tagore's poetry, its values, were all in Amartya's blood. Coupled with the academic influence of his elders at home, the intellectual atmosphere of the school helped shape the razor-sharp intellect Amartya Sen is known for today.

•

"But what is wrong with St. Gregory's School in Dhaka? Why do you want me to study in Santiniketan now?" persisted Babloo.

"You'll see, this school is perfect for you," replied his mother. "I have studied at Santiniketan too, and I know you'll love it. It's very different from the English-medium schools you have studied in earlier. I remember when I was a student here, we used to be thrilled when it rained because most of the classes are held outdoors and they'd get cancelled," his mother said with a laugh, recalling her own childhood.

"The classes are held outside! Wow!" exclaimed a gleeful Babloo.

"Ma," he said after a pause, "Do you think Rabindranath Tagore will meet me?"

"Babloo... don't you remember, you *have* met Tagore many times as a child!"

"I have?"

"You were very young, I suppose you've forgotten. And unfortunately Tagore died a few years ago, in 1941," Amita said sadly. It had been her dream for Babloo to some day meet the man who had helped shape the destiny of not just her family but that of modern India.

Babloo looked downcast. He had heard a lot about the poet who had made India famous all over the world with his writing. His father had told him that Tagore had won the Nobel Prize. Amartya hadn't known what that was then.

•

Professor Amartya Sen even today regrets not having met Rabindranath Tagore when he returned to Santiniketan. But he also feels bittersweet relief that Tagore died before he could witness the Dhaka riots of 1941. He says, "Tagore and his school constantly resisted the narrowly communal identities of Hindus or Muslims or others, and he was, I suppose, fortunate that he died just before the communal killings fomented by sectarian politics engulfed India through much of the 1940s."

Changing the topic, Amita said, "Babloo, did you know it was Tagore who gave you your name, 'Amartya'! Do you know what it means?"

"Yes! Nana told me it means 'immortal'..."but Ma, everyone has to go to God one day, so how can anyone be immortal?"

"Through your work," Amita replied. It was a line she'd heard from her father many times throughout her life. "Even after death, you can be immortal if your work is so good and meaningful that it remains alive in the minds of people."

Babloo piped up, "Ma, I will do something that will make me immortal, just like my name!"

Amita ruffled her young son's hair. "You can do that later, now come in for lunch!" she said with a laugh and turned to walk inside, swinging her red and white cotton sari pallu over her shoulder.

Smiling broadly, Babloo chased his mother, grabbing at her pallu flying in the breeze.

Babloo would remain a faithful son to Amita, even when he had to leave India for foreign shores. Although Amita never left Santiniketan to live with Amartya, physical distance did not diminish their special bond over time. Well into his sixties, Amartya still called his mother every alternate day, and when he received news of his winning the Nobel Prize, she was the first person he called. Amita continued to live in Santiniketan as its *Ashram Kanya* until she passed away at the age of ninety-two.

Just as Amita had hoped and expected, Santiniketan played an important role in shaping her son's inquisitive and contemplative mind. With its emphasis on building curiosity and knowledge rather than grades, Visva-Bharati is where Amartya says he "formed his educational attitudes". In an interview, Sen once said about his alma mater, "Tagore founded Santiniketan with the idea of creating something different from the English-language Raj kind of school. It also differed from the Indian nationalist school. The teaching language was Bengali, and the place was very self-consciously international, with a sense of global culture."

Years later, when he became famous as Professor Amartya Sen, he recalled how one of his teachers had described a classmate of his as "a serious thinker even though her grades are very good." Being an excellent student himself, Visva-Bharati put on him the pressure to prove his worth and wipe away the 'stigma' of his straight A-s!

Santiniketan also laid emphasis on music and drama, especially *Rabindra Sangeet,* but to Amartya it was all a mystery. "I try very hard," he once told his mother after a music lesson, "but I always end up reciting instead of singing." As he grew older, his musical preferences tended more towards jazz and Western classical, and Santiniketan accepted even that!

One of the things that affected Amartya the most while at Santiniketan was the plight of the poor, something he had already begun to notice at a young age whilst in Dhaka. The poverty and hunger that had killed Kader Mian prevailed in Santiniketan as well as in nearby Calcutta. As progressive as Santiniketan was, its students hailed mostly from the privileged classes. In an interview he gave to *The Guardian,* he recalled having seen a man wandering into the campus one day, evidently mentally disturbed and completely starved. To his dismay, instead of helping him and offering him food, most of the other children jeered at him. Amartya, however, struck up a conversation with him and discovered he had not eaten in forty days. He became determined to do all he could to help the deprived. As he became a little older, he began his efforts by conducting evening classes for children from the neighbouring villages. Lalit Majumdar, who taught Amartya English at Santiniketan has to this day preserved a postcard his young student had sent him requesting him for text books and slates for the deprived children he was teaching at a night school in Ballavpur village, two miles away from Santiniketan. "Even as a young boy he had a deep, active and genuine interest in social welfare, especially mass education," Majumdar recalls.

Perhaps the greatest influence on Babloo, that indirectly drove him towards his chosen field of welfare economics, was the aftermath of the Great Bengal Famine of 1943. The famine claimed over two million lives, and Amartya often saw streets lined with animal corpses and the emaciated figures of men, women and children wandering in search of food. Even as a twelve-year-old boy, Babloo had tried to help in his own small way by handing out a can of rice to any starving refugee who passed by his grandfather's house in Santiniketan. His grandfather did not permit him to give more than one can per person, and this troubled Amartya greatly. Perhaps it also helped him realize that starvation was not always a consequence of food shortage but poor food circulation—a theory he would propound later on in life.

In an interview in 1986, he recalled that coming from an intellectual, elite Bengali family, he had not experienced suffering and hunger, but he could never erase the memory of starving people pleading for a few drops of rice starch. He recalled being struck by a tremendous sense of bewilderment. Why was this happening? Who were these people? These questions persisted in the young boy's mind. Describing his feelings at the time, Amartya said, "The main memory that I have of that period is not of my trying to help in a tiny little way, but the opposite. The bewilderment as to why suddenly people were dying in such numbers. Where did they come from? I didn't know any of them. Like all famines, this was a rigidly class-based one. Depending on which occupation group you belonged to, which class you came from, you either got decimated or you had no problem whatsoever. Ninety to ninety-five percent of Bengalis' lives went on absolutely normally, while three million died."

Much later in his life, when Amartya's opinions on poverty were based as much on his sense of compassion as on sound economic theories, he remarked, "Economic unfreedom, in the form of extreme poverty, can make a person a helpless prey to violations of other kinds of freedom." Through his explorations into famines and starvation, he influenced critical national policies on these issues by revealing the clear links between food shortages and government policies.

During his schooling Babloo also developed a deep admiration for India's rich cultural heritage, in which he began to see the perfect foundation for building a modern India. Inculcating a sense of love for one's country while at the same time nurturing an international outlook was the basic principle on which Tagore had founded Santiniketan, and it became the guiding principle of Amartya's life.

In five short years, in 1950, the young Babloo would leave the idyllic environs of Santiniketan and travel to some of the most elite academic circles around the world. But no matter where he went, he remained true to the culture of his homeland and the teachings he received there.

Don't ask what the world needs. Ask what
makes you come alive, and go do it
Because what the world needs is people who
have come alive

— *Howard Thurman* —

3

TRANSFORMATIONS

The Air India flight from London to New Delhi via Geneva had just taken off and all the passengers had settled back for the long journey. Seated towards the rear was a young Bengali man who would one day go on to make history, but on that day he was just another Indian student going home. The twenty-year-old Amartya tried to take a nap but he was returning to India after three years at Trinity College, Cambridge, England and he was too excited to rest.

As he looked out the window at the clouds falling away beneath him, his mind travelled back in time to the journey that had brought him to England.

Amartya had always been a bright child, showing much promise at Santiniketan. Although his interests had largely been academic, he had struggled with deciding which subject to pursue. This was not because he was not interested in any subject but because his areas of interest covered a wide arc. As Johnathan Steele put it in a piece in *The Guardian*, "By then Sen was already bent on an academic career. He knew he wanted to be a teacher or researcher of some sort, though his interests wavered." Says Sen, "I seriously flirted in turn with Sanskrit, mathematics and physics, before settling on the eccentric charms of economics." Explaining his choice, Amartya stated that it was because "economics is also concerned with the poor, the downtrodden, the underdog of society, which is something that is very close to my heart."

After his schooling in Santiniketan, Amartya graduated from Calcutta's Presidency College, one of India's oldest, most eminent colleges. He was there from 1950 to 1953, completing an economics major and a mathematics minor. Calcutta in those days was a deeply leftist, politically charged state and these influences existed within Amartya's own family as well. One of his uncles who belonged to the Congress Socialist Party had been put into preventive detention by the British and spent six years in prison without trial, while another cousin, in the Communist Party, was also in jail. Amartya was thus at the nerve centre of a charged atmosphere that fanned the flame he held within him to do good for society and see it prosper. Yet, as he says, he "could not develop enough enthusiasm to join any political party." Steele analyzed this: "It was an early sign of his detachment from collective action, as well as the pragmatic caution which have stayed with him, in spite of his moral engagement and intellectual boldness."

Alongside, throughout Amartya's time in Calcutta, memories from Dhaka and the Great Bengal Famine remained fresh in his mind. He had been unable to forget the gaunt faces of the hungry who had walked past his house each day. Even in 1951, Calcutta was still full of reminders of that time. There was a deep divide between the elite students of Presidency College and the downtrodden living on the streets around it. Amartya was acutely aware of these differences and of how the economic class to which he belonged had been completely unaffected by the famine even as landless labourers had died by the million. His growing concerns for these economic issues coupled with the charged leftist political atmosphere at Presidency College led Amartya to discover an interest in welfare economics, economic inequality and issues of poverty. Years later, the Royal Swedish Academy of Sciences, which awarded him the Nobel Prize for Economics, would cite his work on these very subjects as having contributed to his receiving the prize.

The seeds of Amartya's brilliant career that had been laid in Santiniketan prospered at Presidency College. Even today, Amartya speaks fondly of his time at Presidency and in particular the influence of his professors, Bhabatosh Datta and Tapas Majumdar, and of his classmates, Sukhamoy Chakravarty and Mrinal Datta Chaudhuri. Chaudhuri was an old friend of Amartya's who had also studied with him in Santiniketan and with whom Amartya's personal and professional association would last a long time. At Presidency, he also forged strong ties with students of its well-known history department who, in his words, helped in "radically broadening" his horizons. He also said, "The educational excellence of Presidency College was captivating. My interest in economics was amply rewarded by quite outstanding teaching."

•

Even as his academic pursuits were sharpening his intellect, Amartya was growing as a human being. Over the course of his life, he was to realize that life is an unending series of ups and downs. It was during his Presidency College days that he had his first experience of this. In early 1952, still just eighteen years old, Amartya started finding it difficult to swallow food and, to his shock, noticed a large lump inside his mouth. Alarmed, he consulted doctor after doctor, all of whom assured him and his parents that it was a benign growth that would heal itself. Amartya however was convinced it was more serious and refused to accept the diagnoses. He relentlessly pursued the doctors until more in-depth tests finally revealed that he was suffering from cancer of the mouth.

Seated in a doctor's clinic, holding the report in her hand, Amartya's mother was devastated.

"Cancer...?" she said softly, in sheer disbelief.

"Mrs Sen, there are treatments we can attempt..." the doctor tried to assure her.

"Attempt? *Attempt?* You're telling me my son has cancer and all you can do is *attempt* some treatment?"

"I'm sorry... but..."

Amartya who had been sitting silently all this while cut him off abruptly. "Come on, let's go home," he said to his mother.

"But Babloo..."

Amartya was already walking out the door.

Amita went home that day a defeated woman, but Amartya's reaction was very different. Even as he had received the diagnosis, he had decided to fight the illness using all the tools he had at his disposal—his aggressiveness, his superior research skills and his refusal to cow down before a challenge. Amartya found out all he could about his condition. His research showed that radiation was a possible line of treatment, though not advised by medical practitioners in those days as it was still not completely understood. Ready to try everything he could, he convinced a doctor at a hospital in Calcutta he later described as "rather primitive" to treat him with a near-fatal dose of radiation. The radical method left him extremely uncomfortable for almost a year but ultimately saved his life. Writing about this, M.C. Munger of Duke University USA states that it was characteristic of Amartya—he was willing to cripple himself rather than submit to despair.

With his health under control, Amartya turned once again to his academic aspirations with renewed faith and spirit.

•

After completing his B.A. from Presidency, Amartya was accepted by Trinity College England for a second B.A., this time in pure economics. Trinity had been established in 1546 by Henry VIII and had produced several prime ministers, heads of state, and Nobel laureates, with Isaac Newton, Francis Bacon and Byron as examples of its prestigious alumni.

At the time Amartya entered its portals, British economists were starkly divided between those for and those opposed to Keynesian economics. These divisions often took on aggressive tones, with debates and differences often turning ugly. In this battle of economists, Trinity was an oasis of sorts, where three esteemed economists from three different schools of thought co-existed peacefully—the Marxist Maurice Dobb, the conservative neo-classicist Dennis Robertson and Piero Sraffa who was essentially skeptical of all schools of thought. Amartya considered himself extremely fortunate to be trained by such remarkable talents.

After graduating at the top of his class in 1956, he stayed on at Trinity for a three-year-long research stint that would lead to the completion of his Ph.D. Amartya's first preference for his thesis topic was the theory of social choice. However, unable to generate enough interest in the subject among his guides and professors, he finally settled on the choice of techniques, a topic that interested Dobb as well as Amartya's brilliant pro-Keynesian guide, Joan Robinson. Perhaps the time for studying social choice had not arrived, but his interest in the topic would lead him back to it many years later.

In 1957, when he had completed just one of the three years allotted to him for his doctoral research, Amartya decided to return home to Calcutta. Confident that the work he'd done that year would be sufficient to result in a thesis, he decided to take a break in India for the remaining two years of his enrollment and now found himself on a flight to Calcutta.

•

Amartya snapped out of his reverie when a stewardess appeared with a tray of food.

"Excuse me, how long until we land?" he asked.

"Not too long now, Sir. Just a little over an hour."

A small smile played on his lips as he looked forward to reaching his country, his city, Calcutta, where he knew his parents would be waiting to receive him.

Although Amartya had no fixed plans of what he would do in Calcutta during his break, he had not imagined taking on a job. Within a few months of arriving, he was made an irresistible offer by Triguna Sen, then education minister of West Bengal, to head the economics department of the newly set up Jadavpur University, close to Calcutta. Amartya was a thoroughbred academic, born on a campus and having lived on campuses all his life with his professor father. Therefore, as he says, "...the idea that I should be a teacher and a researcher of some sort did not vary over the years." Snapping up the opportunity, the twenty-three-year-old Amartya became Professor Amartya Sen and helped set up the economics department from scratch.

Barely older than his students, Amartya's arrival at Jadavpur was at first fiercely protested, then grudgingly accepted and finally embraced wholeheartedly. The professor was once greeted with graffiti on the university walls depicting him as a baby in a cradle, but soon the students and staff alike came to appreciate his brilliance and soft-spoken but firm demeanour.

The professor in Jadavpur was still a PhD student in Trinity, and on the insistence of his guides, Amartya was required to select a supervisor for his thesis. Amartya was never one to pass up the opportunity to increase his span of knowledge. So although he felt his thesis was complete and did not need any external assistance, he chose only the best—the great economic methodologist A.K. Dasgupta who was then teaching at Benaras. The two men went on to forge a friendship and Amartya's time in India was often spent engrossed in conversations with Dasgupta on a wide range of subjects. Once in a while, these conversations would include Amartya's thesis, which he successfully submitted in 1959 to complete his PhD.

But there was yet another important relationship Amartya was to forge while in Jadavpur.

At the College Street Coffee House in Calcutta, one of his favourite restaurants since his student days at Presidency, Amartya turned to his childhood friend Mrinal Datta who was poring over a student's paper while sipping his coffee.

"Mrinal..."

"Hmmm..." he responded, distractedly.

"Mrinal, listen."

"Yes, yes..." he said, continuing to read.

"Mrinal!" Amartya said, loud enough for the young couple at the next table to turn and glance at him.

Surprised to hear his otherwise quiet friend speak with such urgency, Mrinal raised his eyes from the paper and peered at Amartya over his spectacles.

"Yes, I'm listening. What's wrong?"

Amartya fidgeted with his coffee cup.

"Well?"

Hurriedly he said, "Do you remember Nabaneeta?"

"Nabaneeta...?"

"Nabaneeta Dev? That literature student? We ran into her in the cafeteria?"

"Oh, yes, that shy girl with spectacles! Hmm. What about her?"

Amartya paused, apparently at a loss for words, then with nothing else to say, commented, "She's an excellent writer..."

"Okay..." responded Mrinal, a note of uncertainty in his voice.

"Don't you think so?"

"I don't really know Amartya," and with that Mrinal turned back to his work.

"Oh I do...she is. Her professors think she has real potential."

"Okay. That's... excellent."

"There's something about that girl, don't you think?"

What was going on? Mrinal abandoned the idea of finishing his paper, took off his spectacles and set them aside.

"Something...?" he asked, unsure where this was going but sure it was going somewhere.

"You know, something... refreshing. She's not like the others."

"Is she in a class of yours?"

"No, no. In fact, I don't think she has the least bit interest in economics," Amartya said with a short laugh.

As his smile lingered on his lips longer than usual, it

finally struck Mrinal why Amartya could not stop talking about a girl they had barely met a few times.

A wide smile spreading across his face, he said teasingly, "So, has our professor finally found something he likes more than economics?"

Amartya smiled... and that was all it took for Mrinal to realize he had just lost his childhood friend to love.

Daughter of famed Bengali poets Narendra Dev and Radharani Devi, Nabaneeta was a student of comparative literature at Jadavpur University when she first met Amartya. Yet, their paths had crossed several times in the past. Like Amartya, she too had done her B.A. at Presidency College in Calcutta, and her name was also a gift from Rabindranath Tagore. But being five years Amartya's junior, they did not meet until he began teaching at Jadavpur.

With Amartya and Nabaneeta, the romance kindled immediately. Amartya pursued Nabaneeta with the same dedication that he brought to his work, and the young girl could not help but succumb to the charms of the university's favourite (and youngest) professor. Nabaneeta once described herself as feeling at the time like "a dwarf being approached by the moon!"

Despite his growing attraction for Nabaneeta on the one hand, Amartya continued to remain the focused academician. While waiting for the three-year period stipulated by Trinity College for the submission of his thesis, he entered it for a competitive Prize Fellowship at Trinity. As could have been expected, he was selected for the fellowship and now had the choice of continuing to live in Calcutta or returning to Cambridge. Always one for carefully calculated decisions,

Amartya decided to divide his time between the two cities. To initiate the fellowship, he needed to return to Cambridge at once. But first, there was another important decision to take.

Nabaneeta and Amartya had met several times and their relationship was now an open secret on the Jadavpur campus. Whenever he was in the city, Amartya made it a point to drop in at her home at 72, Hindustan Park, and take her out for tea with his friends and colleagues Paramesh Roy and Mrinal Datta Chaudhury. By the time he was to leave for Cambridge, he had made up his mind that the next time he returned, he would take Nabaneeta back with him.

The fellowship gave him four years of freedom to do whatever he wanted. Since Amartya had always been a thinker as much as an economist, his interest in logic and epistemology prompted him to take the radical decision to study philosophy. While some may have perceived this as a complete shift from his study of economics, to Amartya, philosophy was closely related to social choice theory, inequality and deprivation, subjects he had been researching. Further, to him economics was a 'complete' science that included within its purview philosophical logic, ethics and humanitarian values. Aside from these parallels between the two disciplines, Amartya, in his constant hunger for knowledge, also found the study of philosophy rewarding on its own. As he said, "While I am interested both in economics and in philosophy, the union of my interests in the two fields far exceeds their intersection."

It was at this time, in 1959, that Nabaneeta arrived in England glowing from the success of her first book, *Pratham*

Pratyay, a collection of poetry. Amartya received her and took her to Cambridge where the two spent as much time together as they could. On one occasion they went to see Irish playwright Brendan Behan's play *The Hostage*, which was a tremendous success at the time, but so engrossed were they in each other that they didn't wait till the end but left halfway to spend time together by the Thames. A few days later, Amartya formally proposed to her. Says Nabaneeta about the proposal, "I was nonplussed even though my mind was set in tune."

After securing their parents' blessings, they got engaged in Cambridge and were married in India in the summer of 1960. And so the economist-philosopher added 'husband' to his list of accomplishments.

The real voyage of discovery consists
not in seeking new landscapes
but in having new eyes

— *Marcel Proust* —

4

THE NOMADIC ACADEMIC

For all the campuses Amartya had seen, the Trinity College campus to him was one of the most beautiful. Walking down a cobbled pathway past Trinity's famous chapel, he found himself as usual admiring its immaculately trimmed lawns and stunning architecture. As he inhaled the scent of the freshly cut grass, his thoughts meandered to his conversation with Nabaneeta that morning over breakfast.

"So, Nabaneeta, how does it feel being a Harvard Fellow?" he had asked her jovially while buttering his toast. Nabaneeta had recently received a coveted fellowship from Harvard University USA whose alumni included people like John F.

Kennedy and Ralph Waldo Emerson apart from several Nobel laureates.

Nabaneeta could do no more than laugh out loud. She'd had a twinkle in her eye ever since she had received the news, and Amartya was overjoyed at his wife's achievement.

A soccer ball soaring through the air and heading directly for his head interrupted his thoughts. He quickly raised his arms in defence and caught the errant ball.

"Sorry, Prof!" a young boy in jeans and sweatshirt called out to him from across the lawns. Amartya threw the ball back at the group of students playing an impromptu game between classes. "Good catch, Prof!" the boy called out.

Amartya laughed. It was good to know his sporting skills had not faded entirely. With a smile, he turned and continued walking towards his office.

The students' carefree ways took him back to his own early days at Trinity as an undergraduate student in 1953. Returning to the college as a Fellow and professor in 1957 had felt like coming home. But now it was 1960 and, although he still felt fortunate to be at the respected institution, he had to admit Trinity no longer stimulated him as it once did. The economists from various competing schools of thought had attracted him at first, but he now realized the college did not benefit from this unique situation—there were neither heated debates nor a passionate exchange of ideas. Instead, as described by him, the faculty members were "contending armies" involved in "sterile" debates. By the time he reached his office and sank into his leather swivel chair, he had finally admitted to himself that his time at Trinity would have to come to an end soon.

Amartya Sen as a teenager with his sister, Supurna Datta, and a cousin

Amartya Sen with his second wife, Eva Colorni

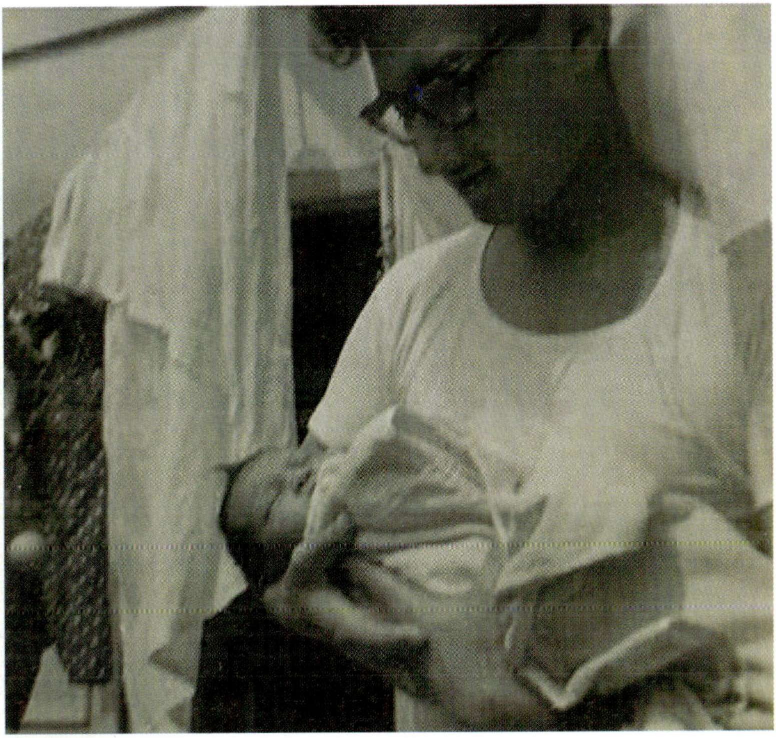

Amartya Sen with his first daughter, Antara Dev Sen, as a baby

Amartya Sen with his first daughter, Antara Dev Sen

Amartya Sen

Amartya Sen taking coffee after lunch at the family home in Santiniketan, Pratichi

Amartya Sen with his wife, four children, and their spouses

Amartya Sen with the long-standing and beloved staff of the family home on Santiniketan, Pratichi

Amartya Sen with his wife, Emma Rothschild

Amartya Sen and Emma Rothschild

Amartya Sen and Emma Rothschild

Amartya Sen with his son, Kabir Sen, his daughter, Indrani Sen, and his wife, Emma Rothschild, at Kabir's wedding

Thinking a temporary change of scene would alter his mind, Amartya took a break from Trinity that same year and went to America for a year-long stint as visiting faculty at the Massachusetts Institute of Technology (MIT). Teaching at MIT until 1961, he was struck by its vibrant academic atmosphere, so unlike Trinity's. Amartya also received tremendous inspiration from his interactions with Paul Samuelson, Robert Solow, Franco Modigliani and others at MIT. His short time there was enough for him to decide to leave Trinity College altogether.

When he broke the news to Nabaneeta, she wasn't too surprised. She had come to realize that even some of the world's most respected universities were too small to contain Amartya's ambitions. Over the years, she accompanied Amartya in his life as a wandering academic of sorts, and throughout their marriage the two often moved back and forth between Trinity, MIT, Stanford, Berkeley, Harvard, Delhi and the London School of Economics (LSE). Speaking of those years, Nabaneeta recalls, "Life was modest but happy in the formative years. We kept on frisking from one place to another."

Continuing the 'frisking', in 1963, Amartya decided to not just leave Trinity but Cambridge itself. Nabaneeta had by then completed her PhD from Newnham College in Cambridge and was expecting their first child, Antara. Amartya was maturing as a man, as a father and certainly as an economist. In his hunger for new horizons, his small but growing family relocated to Delhi, where Professor VKRV Rao had set up the Delhi School of Economics in 1949, with assistance from Prime Minister Jawaharlal Nehru. Professor Rao was instrumental in convincing Amartya that Delhi would provide as much academic stimulation as the British and American universities he had worked in thus far. Amartya, always eager to serve his country, agreed.

•

In Delhi, Amartya discovered a truly dynamic environment, which was also receptive to his interest in social choice—the very topic he had not been allowed to research as a student at Trinity. Excited by the possibilities, he decided to make Delhi his home for a while. But first, he had to fulfil a commitment he had made to visit Berkeley, California, as visiting professor. In 1964, one year after landing in Delhi, Amartya and his wife spent a year at Berkeley before heading back to their country.

Berkeley provided Amartya with the intellectual kickstart he was seeking. While he worked as Associate Professor, his wife pursued a post-doctoral fellow. The year proved to be an important one for the couple. It was here that Amartya finally achieved his goal of writing several papers on issues like welfare economics, economic inequality, poverty and famine—issues that had been troubling him since his school days in Santiniketan. Nabaneeta too found herself busy as she grew involved with the free speech movement unfolding among the students of Berkeley. But while Nabaneeta actively participated in the many student marches, Amartya chose to offer his support from the confines of his office. Ever the academic, he believed in making his opinions known through his pen rather than his voice. Says Amartya about his more passive involvement: "I had… developed more scepticism of what could be achieved by activism without necessarily weakening on the importance of the cause."

This was a stance he had maintained throughout his life. Bengal in the 1950s had been one of the most politically active states in India and Amartya had been under enormous pressure from his family to join a political party. He had refused, even though he was substantially influenced by the Leftist view of selflessness and social equality. He wanted his ideas to impact through intellectual force rather than hands-on activism. This goal Amartya achieved when his research on famines done many years later went on to influence the Indian government's policy on famines.

While at Berkeley, Amartya found himself getting more immersed in social choice theory and by the time he returned to Delhi in 1965 he was charged with ideas and inspiration for his classes as well as for his first book.

•

Till 1971 Amartya held the position of Director of the Delhi School of Economics. During this period, he enjoyed his most fruitful phase professionally as he worked hard on converting the D School (as it is popularly known) into an advanced school of economics with the assistance of economist K.N. Raj. By the time he left Delhi, his hard work had succeeded in making the institution an eminent centre of education for economics and the social sciences in India. Today, the D School comprises departments of economics, geography and sociology, of which the department of economics has been designated a Centre of Advanced Study by the University Grants Commission. Seminars, conferences and workshops are periodically organized by the department and they draw academics from the world over. Prime Minister Dr Manmohan Singh too has been on their faculty.

Amartya's other personal ambition of authoring his first book was achieved while in Delhi, in 1970, with *Collective Choice and Social Welfare*, a path-breaking work that presented his views on social decision-making. In his research for the manuscript, he was greatly aided by a brilliant student of the D School, Prasanta Pattanaik, who was also conducting his own research on voting systems.

At the time, the issue of social choice was argued from two opposing and extreme points of view—the free marketeers' point of view according to which government intervention should end altogether and individuals should be free to choose whatever the market offers, and the statists' point of view, which was that governments must make authoritarian decisions for the people. Amartya however adopted a middle path, stating that there need not be a 'perfect' solution and that the choice of the majority is critical only as long as the voice of the minority is not suppressed.

Although the book was largely completed in Delhi, he credits economist, author and professor of economics at Harvard, Kenneth Arrow, and Harvard Professor John Rawls, for giving him insights and suggestions that helped shape the work. Amartya first heard of Arrow in his Presidency College days through friend and co-student Sukhamoy Chakravarty who had encouraged him to read Arrow's book, *Social Choice and Individual Values* (1951). In it, Arrow demonstrated that any social system that utilizes the voting system, allowing voters to choose between options, suffers from inconsistencies. He showed that the ranking preferences given to different candidates by an individual are not representative of the preferences of the community. Using mathematical calculations Arrow had formally proved that social choice is impossible if the solution is to be based on rational and ethical criteria.

Continuing this thread through his book, Amartya aimed to provide an overview of social choice. In his words, "There were a number of analytical findings to report, but despite the presence of many 'trees' (in the form of particular technical results), I could not help looking anxiously for the forest. I had to come back again to the old general question that had moved me so much in my teenage years at Presidency College: Is reasonable social choice at all possible given the differences between one person's preferences (including interests and judgments) and another's (indeed, as Horace noted a long time ago, there may be 'as many preferences as there are people')?"

Amartya's work on the subject prospered when he was invited by Harvard University to spend a year there as visiting faculty in 1968. The offer came while he was still at the D School. At Harvard, Amartya had the opportunity to teach a class with Kenneth Arrow himself. This was a privilege for Amartya, but it also led to many stories and anecdotes, some interesting and some plain hilarious. On a flight to San Francisco once, when Amartya's neighbour discovered he was a professor at Harvard, he asked him if he had heard of an "apparently interesting" course taught by "Kenneth Arrow, John Rawls and some unknown guy." Amartya smiled and with characteristic humility replied, "Yes, I've heard it's quite good," not revealing that the 'unknown guy' was sitting right next to him.

Amartya also taught another course with Stephen Marglin

and Prasanta Pattanaik, his student from the D School who had joined Harvard too by then. In this course, the three examined the connection between social choice theory and other areas in economics. All of these experiences were laying the foundation for Amartya's continuing research in the field of social choice from 1971 onwards when he would join the esteemed London School of Economics as Professor of Economics.

It was a glorious period for Amartya and Nabaneeta, a time of tremendous creative and personal growth. The couple now had two daughters—Antara and Nandana. Amartya was globally considered a powerhouse of economic theory, and Nabaneeta was laying the foundations of an illustrious career as a poet and writer. However, the years that were to follow would not be as easy.

O to be self-balanced for contingencies!
O to confront nights, storms, hunger,
ridicule, accidents and rebuffs
as the trees and animals do

— *Walt Whitman* —

5

THE PARTING OF WAYS

It was the strong, almost burning antiseptic smell that woke Amartya. Still groggy, he struggled to open his eyes and find his bearings. He was lying flat on a hard bed and when he opened his eyes, squinting, what he saw first was the blankness of a white ceiling. Turning slightly, he saw a tube running into his arm and blinking monitors by his side. Slowly, it came back to him.

•

It was 1971. After the success of his first book, Amartya had become a highly sought after economics expert, and the number of talks he gave and universities that appointed him as visiting faculty increased. He was also hard at work on several research papers to be published in the *Review of Economic Studies* as well as on his next book, *Primary Education in Rural India: Participation and Wastage*. All of this was alongside his continuing responsibilities as Professor of Economics at the Delhi School of Economics.

In the midst of a hectic schedule, Amartya noticed that once again it was getting difficult for him to swallow solid food. At first he ignored the problem but it became worse. Twenty years had passed since he had been given radiation for mouth cancer. Not wanting to worry Nabaneeta or the kids he visited the campus doctor at the Delhi School of Economics without telling them.

The news wasn't good. Initial examinations led the doctor to believe that either the radiation treatment he'd received in Calcutta had destroyed the hard palate of his mouth or, worse, the mouth cancer had resurfaced. And surgery was the only way to tell which one it was.

Coming home that evening, Amartya sat down to have a difficult conversation with Nabaneeta. She was worried but also pragmatic. Amartya's illness had appeared at a time when Nabaneeta too had been suffering from terrible asthma, which was being exacerbated by Delhi's tropical climate. The couple therefore jointly decided it would be best for the entire family to leave Delhi and move to London. Those were the circumstances under which Amartya accepted the offer to join the London School of Economics as Professor of Economics. In 1971, therefore, the wandering academic once again uprooted his family and moved back to the UK.

It was in a London hospital that Amartya now lay, still

waking up from an intensive, seven-hour-long surgery. He had been wheeled in for the surgery with no idea if he was suffering from cancer, which would most likely be fatal, or bone necrosis, a non-fatal side effect of radiotherapy, which was complex but curable.

Amartya became aware of some movement and realized there was someone else in the room. Craning his neck, his eyes fell on a nurse standing at the foot of his bed, her blonde hair glowing in the dim light of the room. He opened his mouth to speak but had to clear his throat. It felt dry and scratchy. The nurse poured him a glass of water from a jug. She helped him raise his head and take a sip.

"My wife…?"

He had barely spoken two words but had to stop. His mouth felt swollen, sore.

He tried again, "Where's my wife?"

He sounded like his mouth was stuffed with cotton wool. He felt like it too.

"Oh, she was exhausted so the doctor sent her home to get some rest. We didn't think you'd wake up so soon. You've had a pretty rough day yourself, Mr Sen," she replied in a crisp British accent.

"Oh…" Amartya replied weakly.

Slowly he raised a hand to touch his throbbing cheek. His mind was in turmoil. What had the doctors found?

"Can you tell me how it went?"

The nurse hesitated, opened her mouth to speak, closed it again and then replied, "I'm sorry, I'm not allowed to say; you must wait for the doctors to come at nine in the morning."

"Nurse... please..."

"Why don't you try to get some rest, Mr Sen? Everything will be all right in the morning."

Was that a hint that the doctors had not found cancer?

"Please, I must know."

The nurse stood there wringing her hands. She was evidently itching to tell him something but protocol was holding her back.

"I promise to look very surprised when the doctors give me the news," he said with a smile.

The nurse smiled despite her apprehension and then said in a reassuring tone, "All right, all right, here we go. They didn't find any cancer, but it is necrosis. They've had to reconstruct your palate, but other than that, you're fine."

Amartya felt the tension drain out of his body. He smiled as best he could. "Thank you so much..." he whispered, after which he leaned back on his pillow, once again drifting away into a drugged sleep.

•

When Nabaneeta arrived the following morning, he could see the concern on her face.

"Don't worry," he whispered to her, just as the doctors walked in. Nabaneeta averted her gaze from his and turned to look at the doctors. When they had delivered the good news and left, she stood still for a moment, looking visibly relieved, then walked out of the room saying, "I'll get you some coffee."

Amartya's health was now of less concern to him than his marriage. He could no longer deny that Nabaneeta was unhappy and that their relationship, once loving and romantic, was falling apart in the face of the realities of life. He remembered the time, early in their courtship, when the two had ducked out of a play just to be alone together. Today, however, they could barely be in the same room without an argument or, worse, a stony silence.

Nabaneeta's reputation as a writer had been growing. Since her marriage, she had also completed her post graduation with distinction from Harvard University and obtained a PhD in comparative literature from Indiana University in 1963. Known by now for her feminist writings, she was growing tired of taking a back seat in her own life. She no longer wished to simply follow Amartya from campus to campus, running the household and raising the children. Moreover, during the last few years the couple had been struggling to make ends meet. "We could hardly save a penny those days. Amartya was a good economist but a bad money manager," she said many years later. The economics guru to many was aided in his household economics by friend and colleague Romesh Ganguly who often loaned Amartya money and even helped him stick to a rigorous monthly budget.

When asked about what kind of father Amartya was, Nabaneeta laughingly described him as "a clumsy one until the children grew old enough to be his students."

•

By the end of 1971, the inevitable happened. Nabaneeta and Amartya separated. The separation created a storm of controversy, especially when Nabaneeta returned to Jadavpur as a single mother with two young daughters. But the writer was not just a feminist on paper and she faced it all with grit. In London, Amartya went on to have a successful tenure at LSE till 1977. Nabaneeta meanwhile dedicated her time to her career as a professor and writer alongside raising her children. Throughout the 1970s, she published several novels, children's books and poetry collections, becoming one of the most prominent and prolific Bengali writers of her time. She received many awards for her work, including the Padmashree in 2000, and was invited as visiting faculty by universities like Harvard, Cornell, and British Columbia.

Looking back at the relationship, Nabaneeta only has fond memories. "Over the years I've developed a sense of detachment, but the warmth and goodwill are still there," she says graciously. She continues to enjoy a friendship with Amartya, which has only matured over the years. In fact, in 1998, when he was appointed Master of Trinity College (the first Asian to head an Oxbridge college) it was to Nabaneeta that he first broke the news. When in India, Amartya always visits her, and Nabaneeta too has spent time with Amartya and his second wife Emma Rothschild at their Cambridge home. When Amartya won the Nobel Prize, Nabaneeta's phone was ringing off the hook with people congratulating her!

The perfect gentleman, Amartya describes his ex-wife as "one of the best-known literary names in Bengal, a leading poet and novelist" who he says taught him a lot about poetry. Nabaneeta truly lives up to her image as an admirable woman who has never let life's struggles bring her down, and it is easy to see why Amartya chose to spend the most formative years of his life with her.

His two daughters with Nabaneeta — Antara and Nandana — also visit him often. Today, Antara is a journalist and editor of a literary, political and cultural magazine in Delhi called the *Little Magazine*, a project she started after completing a Reuter Foundation Fellowship from Oxford. Her sister Nandana is a film director, model and actor.

Having been brought up by Nabaneeta in India, but retaining a closeness to their father who travelled around the world, both girls have grown up calling many cities home. Their hearts however are rooted in the same earth as their father's. Nandana especially has a close bond with Santiniketan where she has spent many summers with her grandmother, Amita Sen. According to Amita, Nandana is the one who has inherited her genes –the rest of the Sen clan comprises academics while Nandana has followed in Amita's footsteps, living a life of art, dance and drama.

•

Sir George Bernard Shaw once said, "Difficulties strengthen the mind as labour does the body." Though life was not exactly a bed of roses for Amartya, he went on to achieve goals that perhaps at one time even he did not imagine he could.

Courage and perseverance have a magical talisman, before which difficulties disappear and obstacles vanish into air

— *John Quincy Adams* —

6

SOCIAL CHOICE IN LONDON

Amartya stood silently in his kitchen listening to the sound of his coffee machine. A shaft of sunlight slanted across the wooden floor. It was an unusually sunny day in London. He stared down at his bare feet. He was all by himself, and the new silence was strange but also welcome. He remembered how until just a few months ago, the house would be filled with the constant din of his two young daughters and his wife chasing after them to drink their milk or finish a meal. He'd have such trouble concentrating on work. Now he had the house all to himself.

Nabaneeta had left for Jadavpur a few months ago and Amartya had had to get used to doing things on his own.

She'd always taken care of the food and house, but here he was brewing his own coffee, cooking his own meals. He felt a sense of sadness that the marriage had not worked out, but he also felt a sense of freedom and promise. Both for himself as well as for Nabaneeta. The two had always been far too independent, too focused on their goals to flow with the vagaries of life. And standing in his silent kitchen, now all his own, he looked at his life ahead with this optimism.

Picking up his cup of coffee, he turned to walk back into his study.

•

After 1971, Amartya immersed himself in his work at the London School of Economics, conducting in-depth research on the issue closest to his heart at the time—social choice. Alongside, throughout the '70s, he also wrote a staggering number of journal articles on a range of topics spanning the fields of economics and philosophy such as "Rationality and Morality", "The Concept of Efficiency", "The Labour Theory of Value", "Famine as Failures of Exchange Entitlements". He also attended numerous conferences and symposia as speaker and published his books, *Guidelines for Project Evaluation, Employment, Technology, and Development* and *On Economic Inequality,* which was hugely successful and re-published in several languages. The book explained the relation between social choice theory and welfare economics, Amartya's two areas of specialization, and is still considered essential reading for economists the world over.

The '70s turned out to be the perfect time for Amartya to be researching social choice, and London, the perfect place.

The city was host to a vast number of economists, researchers, historians and academicians from various fields, many of who lived in Amartya's own neighbourhood.

Amartya found inspiration and assistance in his work from some brilliant colleagues such as Peter Hammond, Charles Blackorby, Kotaro Suzumura, Geoffrey Heal, Gracieda Chichilnisky, Ken Binmore, Wulf Gaertner, Eric Maskin, John Muellbauer, Kevin Roberts and Susan Hurley, all of whom were working on social choice problems. LSE also gave him the platform to collaborate with social choice theorists from around the world, including Claude d'Aspremont and Louis Gevers from Belgium, Koichi Hamada and Ken-ichi Inada from Japan and others from countries as far flung as Israel, Australia and Russia.

Although the London School of Economics is where Amartya's work on social choice matured, he never fails to give credit to his colleagues and students at the Delhi School of Economics, where his work in the field first started, in particular to Prasanta Pattanaik, his student who he also worked with at Harvard and with whom he co-authored articles on social choice. He also remembers fondly his close friend and co-student at Presidency College, Sukhamoy Chakravarty, who first introduced him to social choice by encouraging him to read Kenneth Arrow's *Social Choice and Individual Values*. Sukhamoy became a member of the Planning Commission (1971–77) and Chairman of the Economic Advisory Council to the Prime Minister of India. He was India's foremost economist on matters of macro-economic planning and policy. When Sukhamoy died an untimely death in 1990, at the age of 56, Amartya found himself remembering the image of his friend sitting before him at the College Street Coffee House near Presidency, next to a window, sipping coffee and passionately discussing his interpretation of Arrow's work. The image would often return to haunt Amartya over the years.

In his characteristically modest manner Amartya shares credit for his work with many but it is a fact that his work on social choice through the '70s helped shape many of the theories considered axiomatic today. Although social choice came into prominence through the work of Kenneth Arrow, Amartya's contribution to the field was in revealing the conditions under which Arrow's 'Impossibility Theorem' comes to pass and in extending the theory. In doing so, he was in part aided by his interest in and knowledge of philosophy, a seemingly unlikely (at the time) subject he had studied on a fellowship from Trinity College, Cambridge.

The Impossibility Theorem states that any voting mechanism offering three or more ranked preferences can never be based on any reasonable set of criteria. This is a basic manifestation of the concept of social choice and was the springboard from which Amartya began his own investigations into the subject.

To explain what social choice is precisely, it is best to use Amartya's own words extracted from his Nobel Prize acceptance speech. "Social choice theory is a very broad discipline, covering a variety of distinct questions." It is a framework for understanding how individual decisions and preferences aggregate towards the decisions and preferences of the collective. It contains within itself the aggregation of "economic assessment and policy making related to poverty, inequality, unemployment, national income and living standards." Thus, it is a blend of elements from welfare economics and voting theory.

In attempting to explain the relevance of social choice, Amartya cited the old joke, "a camel is a horse designed by a committee," demonstrating how decisions taken by a few rarely reflect the needs of the many. In an effort to ensure that all possible needs are met, a committee may end up with a camel, when the real solution is a horse. In most cases, however, they end up with a centaur perhaps, representing an odd mix of features that prove useless to everyone. Now imagine the committee is the government and the people it represents run into the millions. The government's ability to meet all of their needs becomes even less possible. This is the crux of social choice theory, which asks the question: how is it possible to arrive at an aggregate opinion given the extreme diversity of a large population?

Amartya further explains, "If there is a central question that can be seen as the motivating issue that inspires social choice theory, it is this: how can it be possible to arrive at cogent aggregative judgments about the society (for example, about 'social welfare', or 'the public interest', or 'aggregate poverty'), given the diversity of preferences, concerns, and predicaments of the different individuals *within* the society? How can we find any rational basis for making such aggregative judgements as 'the society prefers this to that', or 'the society should choose this over that', or 'this is socially right'?"

Summarizing the concept of social choice, Amartya once stated at a civic reception given in his honour in Calcutta, "...it addresses the discipline of systematically arriving at social decisions on the basis of the disparate interests and preferences of different members of the society, who come from different classes, distinct communities, dissimilar economic and social backgrounds, divergent cultural and religious beliefs and so on."

Amartya's analysis of this question led him to work on other related issues such as the causation and prevention of famines and hunger, the forms and consequences of gender equality as well as poverty and deprivation.

How are these topics related? In the case of poverty, for instance, social choice theory questions the adequacy of measuring poverty by measuring the number of people living below the poverty line, that is, the head count measure. Imagine a person with an income well above the poverty line who is suffering from a serious kidney disease and requires dialysis. If a person's income is converted into his capability to lead a minimally acceptable life, the lack of appropriate medical opportunities may prevent the person from doing so, resulting in poverty. In other words, deprivation is ultimately related to the lack of opportunities, which can be influenced by numerous factors including personal income, environmental and physical characteristics and other variables like the availability of medical facilities. Thus, poverty can be visualized as serious deprivation in the form of illiteracy, lack of basic health care, under-nourishment etc. This approach presents a picture of poverty different to that yielded by purely income-based analyses.

While Kenneth Arrow demonstrated the occurrence of impossibility in social choice, Amartya found this view "pessimistic" and argued against it by presenting conditions under which impossibility can be overcome. He attempted to show how societies can find ways to make outcomes related to the aggregation of individual choices more accurate. In doing so, he once illustrated Arrow's theory through a cake division problem wherein each person in a group is only concerned with how large his slice is, not caring about the other's share, showing incongruity in social choice. However, he illustrated the unanimity of social choice through the example of a democratic government that has not performed well and is collectively voted out by the general public.

Thus, Amartya stated that although democratic decisions can be at times associated with incongruities, impossibility in social choice can be overcome by utilizing a broad base of information through interpersonal comparisons. These comparisons include both formal reasoning about postulated propositions as well as an informal understanding of values and norms. Formal reasoning must deal with the compatibility and coherence of the proposal, whereas informal reasoning must consider its relevance and apparent validity. Both formal and informal reasoning complement each other and are equally essential.

In a paper titled "Rationality and Social Choice" presented to the American Economic Association, Amartya showed that the use of reasoning and rational assessment has played a major role in eliminating inaccuracies in the aggregation of opinions that may characterize many societies and can help in improving the quality of life.

Showing how far research in the field has come, Amartya once stated at a civic reception held in his honour, "The field of social choice theory looks quite different now, with plenty of possibilities of being constructive and positive in doing socially relevant measurement as well as systematically examining and scrutinizing aggregative judgments about social welfare, poverty and inequality, and about the rights and liberties, and asymmetries of power and opportunities. Indeed, instead of the old question, 'Is it possible to have socially rational decisions based on the interests and preferences of the members of the society?' the new question that has to be addressed is 'Which of the various ways of making socially rational decisions best serve our values of equity and justice?' The choice is no longer just something or nothing, but between many different ways of evaluation among which we can choose by invoking foundational notions such as justice or fairness. Even the apparently technical subject of choosing a suitable measure of poverty for a nation or a state can be seen in terms of the competing values which can be reflected in different ways by distinct statistical measure. It is this linking of knowledge with practice that is perhaps the most encouraging implication of the recent works in welfare economics and social choice theory, including the evaluation of inequality and poverty."

•

It was on studying these issues that Amartya spent much of the '70s. Looking back, he describes that time as "the golden years of social change theory" and himself at that time as "having a ball". So therapeutic and positive was the effect of Amartya's work on him that he made a full recovery, both physically and emotionally. By 1973 he had started living with Eva Colorni, also a brilliant economist teaching at the City of London Polytechnic (now part of the London Metropolitan University). In 1978, the couple married.

Like Amartya, Eva had been raised in a primarily academic environment as the daughter of academic philosopher Eugenio Colorni and writer Ursula Hirschman. Eva's stepfather, Altiero Spinelli, was a statesman and founder of the European Federalist Movement. She herself had studied law, philosophy and economics in Pavia, Italy, and in Delhi before becoming an economics lecturer. Amartya described her as having had a background that "involved a fine mixture of theory and practice."

In Eva, Amartya found an intellectual partner with whom he was able to discuss the nuances of his work. According to him, "She exercised a great influence on the standards and reach that I attempted to achieve in my work (often without adequate success)." Eva especially encouraged Amartya to broaden the range of his work on social choice and use it to assess poverty, to develop distribution-adjusted national income measures, to clarify the penalty of unemployment, to analyze violations of personal liberties and basic rights and to characterize gender disparities and women's relative disadvantage.

And so Amartya moved from strength to strength, and in 1977 decided to leave the London School of Economics and join Oxford University, first as Professor of Economics at Nuffield College and later as Drummond Professor of Political Economy at All Souls College. Despite his move to Oxford, Amartya continued to live in London, a city he had grown to love. There his work branched out in new and unexpected directions.

Banish the mysticism of inequality and you banish almost all the evils attendant on human nature

— *Joel Barlow* —

7

THE MANY FACES OF GENDER INEQUALITY

One sunny morning in the spring of 1983, Amartya was seated in his makeshift office in a village near Calcutta. The Oxford professor had swapped his trademark tweed jacket and baggy corduroys for lighter cotton pants and an open-necked shirt more suited to the Indian weather. As the ceiling fan above his head made more of a noise than a breeze, Amartya tried to focus on the report he was studying. He reached for a handkerchief to mop his brow when the old black telephone on his desk delivered a loud ring. Mildly annoyed at the disturbance, he picked up the receiver to hear the voice of his research assistant at the other end.

"Yes, what is it?" he asked patiently.

"Sir, you'll need to come down to the camp. There's a crisis, and we're in need of your expertise." Amartya could hear the smile in the voice at the other end.

"Excuse me?" They have an economics-related crisis? he wondered.

"Sir, there's a child here who bites every hand within the reach of her teeth! Only you can handle him. You know how good you are with the trouble makers..."

Laughing, Amartya said, "All right, hang on, I'll be right there."

Amartya had only recently arrived in West Bengal from Oxford along with colleague Sunil Sengupta on two important missions—the first was to re-visit his alma mater, the Visva-Bharati at Santiniketan, as visiting faculty for one year. The second was to weigh and study as many children as they could up till the age of five years in two villages of West Bengal to further his study on gender inequality. In doing so, the able economist had discovered a hidden skill—his ability to cajole protesting children into getting weighed without a fuss, and was therefore often called upon by his assistant to help!

Coming to Bengal had helped Amartya further his work on social choice, which he was deeply involved in with the aid of his new colleagues at Oxford as well as his wife, Eva. As his interests shifted from social choice theory to more practical issues related to it, he benefited from the long discussions he often had with her. Amartya graciously credits Eva with being a strong influence on his work at the time, describing her as "deeply humane, with a great passion for social justice, as well as fiercely rational, taking no theory for granted, subjecting each to reasoned assessment and scrutiny."

It was Eva who encouraged Amartya to shift towards analyzing the practical issues related to social choice. Says Amartya, "Her critical standards were extremely exacting, but she also wanted to encourage me to work on issues of practical importance." With her encouragement, Amartya extended his work on social choice and related it to a larger variety of problems. The results of these economic explorations were published in several journals and later compiled into two collections of articles—*Choice, Welfare and Measurement* published in 1982 and *Resources, Values and Development* published in 1984.

Other than poverty and famines some other areas, such as in which Amartya especially focused were not necessarily considered the domain of economists, education and gender equality. Relating all of these fields to his core research area of social choice, Amartya has said, "The reach and relevancc of social choice theory can be very extensive indeed." It is his branching out into these topics of social interest that has earned Amartya the title, 'The Mother Teresa of Economics.'

He was one of the few economists to study gender equality. As a topic, it was considered absurd by most people in the 1960s when he first began his research. Through his work, however, Amartya has time and again proved that economics is not just a subject of academic contemplation but can apply to the daily lives of people. Perhaps gender equality was a subject he felt rather strongly about, being not just a socially aware, liberal economist but also a father of two daughters.

Initially, Amartya's research was confined to analyzing the available statistics on the male-female differential sex ratio in

India. Subsequently, in 1982, he co-wrote a paper with Jocelyn Kynch entitled "Indian Women: Well-being and Survival". He soon widened the scope of his research to conduct international comparisons in books such as *Commodities and Capabilities* published in 1985 as well as some general theories regarding gender inequality as published in *Gender and Cooperative Conflict* in 1990.

It was in this regard that, in 1983, he arrived in India with Sunil Sengupta to conduct first-hand research. Their findings were compiled as a paper entitled "Malnutrition of Rural Children and Sex Bias", which was published in the *Economic and Political Weekly* in 1983. In two villages of West Bengal, the pair compared male and female babies up to the age of five years and, in Amartya's words, he "developed some vanity in being able to meet the challenge at the 'biting end' of social choice research"!

Through his research, Amartya concluded that from a biological point of view, female infants are stronger than male infants, that is, nature exhibits a natural preference for the female sex. Despite this fact, on an average, globally, there are only about 98 women for every 100 men. This female to male sex ratio is even more lopsided in poor countries like India (93:100) and Bangladesh (94:100). Wealthier nations such as Europe and North America, on the other hand, have a female to male ratio of 05:1 or an average of 105 women per 100 men. Amartya closely studied this 'shortfall' of women in some countries and coined the term 'missing women' in an article he wrote in the *British Medical Journal* in 1992, referring to women who are not alive due to neglect and discrimination.

He claimed that this lopsided male to female ratio in developing parts of Asia and North Africa results from boys receiving better health treatments and opportunities. Along with his academic collaborator Jean Drèze, a Belgian economist, Amartya proposed that there were over 100 million such 'missing women' who had died as a result of unequal access to resources in the developing world. In a subsequent debate, he refined these estimates using different demographic techniques. In his seminal paper on the subject published in the *British Medical Journal,* he cited yet another cause for these women going 'missing'. He said, "There have been two opposite movements: female disadvantage in mortality has typically been reduced substantially, but this has been counterbalanced by a new female disadvantage—that in natality—through sex specific abortions aimed against the female fetus. The availability of modern techniques to determine the sex of the fetus has made such sex selective abortion possible and easy, and it is being widely used in many societies." However, today, the governments of many Asian countries where sex-selective abortions are common are trying to minimize their incidence; for instance, the PCPNDT (pre-conception pre-natal diagnostic test) Act has been implemented in India.

Amartya worked on problems of discrimination against women in the development process and on survivorship differentials between men and women under conditions of social discrimination against women. He discussed the rising rate of women's mortality due to poor health opportunities for women and the undernourishment of girls, resulting in an increased prevalence of low birth weight. In South Asia, for instance, nearly 21 per cent of children are clinically underweight at the time of birth. This results in a vicious cycle wherein undernourished mothers give birth to low-birth-weight babies who suffer from the repercussions of gender inequality and grow to become undernourished mothers themselves.

Besides this, women in many developing countries are sometimes not even provided with basic facilities like education and are discouraged from developing their natural talents or freely participating in the social functions of the community. Afghanistan may be the only country in the world where girls are even barred from attending school.

Even in terms of employment and promotions at workplaces, women are discriminated against. In a progressive country like Japan where women receive equal facilities, they are still not given equal employment opportunities. Further, in many societies, the ownership of property and the right to the inheritance of basic assets such as a home and land may be very unequal. This absence of the right to property can prevent women from entering and flourishing in commercial, economic and social activities.

This type of inequality has existed in most parts of the world, though there are local variations. For example, even though in major parts of India property is inherited exclusively by males, in the states of Kerala and Meghalaya, the system of matrilineal inheritance for an influential section of the community, including the Nair community, is common.

Gender inequality is often apparent even in so-called 'modern' households when it comes to a husband and wife sharing the burden of housework and childcare, though there may be no obvious signs of discrimination against women.

Amartya attempted to devise an economic model that would help negate the neglect of women and remove gender inequality. He discussed in this context the experience in the state of Kerala, which is a sharp contrast to many other parts of India in that it has little or no gender inequality in terms of mortality. Indeed, not only is the life expectancy of women in Kerala over 76 (compared with 70 for men), the female-male ratio of Kerala's population is 06:1 (106 women for every 100 men). Some of the factors that have led to this empowerment of women are the high level of women's literacy in the state, greater access of women to well-paid and well-respected jobs and a decline in the fertility rate. All these factors along with women's right to inherit property in Kerala are interlinked and help in the overall empowerment of women. Similar changes can be observed in other parts of India where women's empowerment has increased with greater literacy besides economic and social involvements outside the home.

With all of these facts, it may appear as if gender inequalities exist only in developing countries. This is an incorrect assumption and Amartya showed how it exists in various forms all over the world. Western countries like the USA and the UK too suffer from gender inequalities, albeit in different forms. For example, as Amartya stated, though Asian countries like India, Bangladesh, Pakistan and Sri Lanka have had female heads of governments at various points of time in their political history, no woman has been head of government in the USA. Another example Amartya cites is from his days as professor at the Delhi School of Economics where he found a larger proportion of women holding important posts in the college faculty than he saw either at Harvard University or at Trinity College, Cambridge.

In more recent times, Amartya has furthered his work on gender inequality to show how it affects not just women but men as well. According to him, while women should be treated equally purely by virtue of being human beings, it may also be worthy to remember that, as he says, "the penalty of gender inequality is paid not only by women but also by men." Unequal treatment to women usually manifests as unequal access to medical treatment. As women grow physically weaker, the health of the children they bear is affected in turn. These health issues follow these children well into their old age. Amartya explains: "It turns out that women's maternal undernourishment often leads to fetal distress. One effect of that is seen not just among the children when they're born, neonatal or older children, but decades later in the lives of people in their being more vulnerable to cardiovascular diseases. This is a connection which has emerged from the works of a number of English doctors in particular, led by Professor D.J.P. Barker of Southampton University. It's not surprising that for example the South Asian population, where maternal undernourishment is high, where women's neglect of health care and nutrition is also quite high, also happens to have the highest case of cardiovascular diseases, even after correcting for the economic and social factors that might influence it. This shows that the reach of gender inequality often penalizes men, because it's men who are much more vulnerable to cardiovascular diseases than women are."

In a hard hitting remark, Amartya said, "I don't believe in God, but if I did, one could see almost a divine retribution that you neglect women and they ultimately hit back on men in terms of contributing to greater cardiovascular ailments in late life."

Over the years, researchers have attempted to present alternate theories to explain 'missing women'. However, Amartya's theory has stood the test of time and is, till date, considered the strongest explanation for the phenomenon. No surprise then that by this point in his career, Amartya was considered one of the world's leading experts on his topics of research and was a celebrity of sorts in academic circles.

•

But life also had some more difficulties in store for Amartya. He received a major blow when Eva died from stomach cancer in 1985. She left behind two children, Indrani (ten years old) and Kabir (eight), who Amartya was now solely in charge of. He made the best parenting decision he could at the time and decided to not just move cities but move countries, so that his children would not constantly feel their mother's absence. In 1988, therefore, the Sen family left England and moved to a new campus, this time to Harvard University in America, which he joined as professor of economics and philosophy and as a Senior Fellow at the Harvard Society of Fellows.

In Amartya's mind and heart Eva lived on. Following her death, he instituted a series of lectures known as The Colorni Lectures, which are regularly held at the London Guildhall University in her memory. Amartya is a regular contributor to these lectures.

Now a single parent, Amartya began to worry about his

children who were being raised within his academic world—a world that was wide in some aspects but limited in others. The children were extremely familiar with campuses all over North America, but their knowledge of the country outside was somewhat limited. Amartya confesses to being more worried than amused when on a flight to San Francisco he once overheard the then nine-year-old Kabir asking, "Is that city closer to Palo Alto or to New Haven?" in response to a friendly American who had asked if he knew where Washington DC was.

The city of Palo Alto in the state of California is located thirty-five miles south of San Francisco, which is famous for Stanford University. The city of New Haven located in the state of Connecticut is best known as the home of Yale University. Kabir at the age of nine knew more about America's campus cities than its capital!

As a father, Amartya was somewhat concerned about imposing his lifestyle on his children, but as an economist, he had little to worry about. From gender inequality, at Harvard began his next economic investigation, this time into the causes and effects of famines. The theories he went on to develop are today among the most noted in the field.

Times of general calamity and confusion
have ever been productive of the greatest minds. The
purest one is produced from the
hottest furnace and the brightest thunderbolt is elicited
from the darkest storms

— *Charles Caleb Colton* —

8

THE GREAT BENGAL FAMINE

"Starvation is the characteristic of some people not *having* enough food to eat. It is not the characteristic of there *being* not enough food to eat." So begins Amartya Sen's book, *Poverty and Famines* (1981), an essay on "entitlement and deprivation".

Witnessing the toll that the Great Bengal Famine of 1943 took on the citizens of Bengal, while still only ten years old, Amartya had wondered about how his grandfather allowed him to give only one tin of rice to each starving family wandering the streets, begging for food. The Sens were one of the many rich families that were unaffected by the famine and they certainly had enough rice for themselves. So why just one tin?

As an economist, many decades later, Amartya analyzed this phenomenon of the existence of sufficient food, yet some segments of society starving due to lack of access to it. What had caused this famine in Bengal that resulted in millions dying of starvation? Was it also a case of food being in existence but just not being available to the starving masses? How many people really died? The answers to these questions can be found in the numerous books, papers and speeches Amartya has presented on famines, poverty, starvation and the inter-relations between the three, often using the Bengal Famine of 1943 as a case in point. His research on famines began in all seriousness in the mid-1970s. This is also when he began to work in conjunction with the World Employment Programme of the International Labour Organization, for which he wrote *Poverty and Famines.*

By the late '70s, he also began to devote a serious amount of time exploring social choice problems related to individual advantage. In 1979, he delivered a series of lectures on this topic as visiting faculty at Stanford. These lectures came to be known as the Tanner Lectures and were later published as *Equality of What?* in 1980 and again in 1987. Amartya describes these lectures as an attempt to understand "individual advantage not merely as opulence or utility, but primarily in terms of the lives people manage to live and the freedom they have to choose the kind of life they have reason to value. The basic idea here is to pay attention to the actual 'capabilities' that people end up having. The capabilities depend both on our physical and mental characteristics as well as on social opportunities and influences and can thus serve as the basis not only of assessment of personal advantage but also of efficiency and equity of social policies."

A natural teacher, Amartya had a way of bringing to life even the most staid economic theories. His classes were never entirely formal affairs, and he encouraged interaction and discussion over a one-way imparting of information. This is how Amartya had been educated once in the small town of Santiniketan and this is the teaching style he took with him around the world to the biggest universities.

Standing at the dais, Amartya read from his notes in his distinctive accent—a result of the many years he had spent in London mixed with the after-effects of radiation therapy. "The city of Chittagong was once a profitable seaport in present-day Bangladesh, lush with green paddy fields. It was in many ways the village ideal of India, but it underwent a drastic and unfortunate transformation. The green fields became barren land, villages seemed lifeless and the clusters of mud houses inhabited by poor labourers—fishermen, agricultural labourers, craftsmen—now stood empty. Nothing remained after the Great Bengal famine of 1943."

"The famine had shown the most heartless discrimination. While the middle and upper classes had been left unaffected, it had worst affected those who were bitterly poor even in good times, for whom living hand to mouth was a daily affair. Now, their condition had gone from bad to worse."

From the very back of the large auditorium-style classroom, a student spoke up in a thick accent Amartya recognized as South East Asian, "When you say the poorest… which classes or communities do you mean?"

"The people who died were primarily rural wage earners working and cultivating fields, but also wageworkers in river transport, minor trade and minor services like barbers and craftsmen producing crafts to sell, for none of which there was a market once the famine hit. Famine is a subject in which class-based analysis, as you will see, is very helpful."

"Now, a man can live without a roof over his head or clothes on his body, but a man cannot live without food, and this is the one basic need of life that the famine stole. The wholesale price of rice, the staple diet of most of the population of Calcutta, sky-rocketed from Rs 13 per maund, which is about 82.3 lb or 37 kg, in December 1942… you might want to make a note of these figures… to Rs 21 per maund in March 1943 and to above Rs 30 by May. Although there are no official figures for further price hikes, unofficial reports state that in some places, the price was as high as Rs 80 to Rs 108 per maund. Now these classes we spoke of could previously barely afford the six rupees to keep themselves and their families fed, and the new prices for them were totally out of reach. They began to do the only thing they could."

"It began with frequent hunger and rampant malnutrition. Hunger strikes and the looting of paddy stores were reported in districts around Calcutta. The honest ones began selling anything they could—small pieces of land, old ploughs, cattle, utensils. When that did not bring in enough money, they began migrating to larger cities in search of jobs and food, but in most cases they failed to find either. Nearly

3.5 lakh families became destitute. With no other alternative, by late 1943, millions were left to starve to death with their families. By September, the disposal of dead bodies had become a problem. By December, even after supplies came in, there was no hope of saving those who were suffering from the after-effects of starvation. The Great Bengal Famine was one of the worst famines in the history of the world, and it claimed the lives of approximately two to three million people."

A young girl with straight black hair and a serious face interrupted Amartya, "But, Professor, official estimates of the deaths are much lower at about one million deaths. Maybe just a little more?"

"Yes, that's an important point," Amartya responded. "The official estimates, as these things usually go, were much lower than the truth. You see, my initial estimates were about three million but it is possible that I overestimated it somewhat. On the basis of later statistics it would seem that a more acceptable number is somewhat lower than that, like two to two and a half million."

Nodding, the girl hunched over her notebook and scribbled the figures in.

Amartya continued. "Now why did so many people die?"

"They couldn't afford to buy food," a student replied emphatically.

"Yes, true. But the problem was not *only* of affordability. The harsh reality is that these people may not have found food to eat even if they'd had the money and the jobs to support them. Remember, a famine is the condition of people not having enough to eat, not necessarily a condition of there not being enough to eat."

"But the most common cause of the famine always cited is that India was reeling from World War II and so food production fell drastically?"

"This is also true. Let's examine this first. It is fact that in 1942, when the famine started, India was still five years away from freedom from British rule. World War II was at its peak, and India had been forced into the war by its rulers. When England suffered a disastrous defeat in Singapore against the Japanese army, it was forced to relinquish its hold over Burma, which is now known as Myanmar. This hit India's rice import."

"Why was Burma relevant to rice?" another student asked.

"Burma at that time was one of the largest exporters of rice and India received nearly 15 per cent of its overall rice requirement from there. And, remember, Bengal was geographically situated close to Burma and so it tended to receive the major share of this produce. Now with the Japanese invading Burma, the import of rice obviously stopped. The British authorities were afraid Japan would invade India through Bengal. And whatever rice *was* available to India was being hoarded by the British for their troops in Middle East and Ceylon, which is now Sri Lanka. Indians were going hungry for a war that was not even theirs."

"Professor, is it fair to blame the British? Surely just the vagaries of a war-time situation would contribute to food shortage as well? I mean, that's what happens during a war, right? Prices go up, production declines?"

"Of course, in economics as in any science, we can almost never ascribe the reason of a phenomenon as complex as famine to only one cause in isolation. The 'vagaries of war-time situations' as you put it was certainly another cause of the shortage. There was a war going on. So of course there was a general sense of uncertainty and fear, and what is the one thing people do when they're afraid?"

"Hoard?" the student said tentatively.

"Exactly... rumour mongering can always be expected during times of tension, especially given that there were also air raids in Chittagong, and its first outcome is usually the hoarding of essential supplies. In Bengal, 'essential' equals rice."

"And of course it was the richer folks who got most of the share..." a boy said wryly.

"Unfortunately, yes. The middle and upper classes started purchasing more rice than they needed. Even the government publicly urged the people to buy and save at least two months' stock in their homes. As a result, the price of rice increased disproportionately to a level far beyond the reach of the poor man."

"The problem was compounded when the weather struck against Bengal. On October 16, 1942, the east coasts of Bengal and Orissa were hit by a cyclone, resulting in the flooding of extensive areas of land under rice cultivation and the destruction of the autumn *rabi* crop."

"So what exactly was the government doing through all this?"

"Now we need to understand the mood of the country at that time. There were major political developments taking place in Bengal after the launch of the Quit India movement by the Congress and the communal strife. The government was stretched and simply did not have the resources to pay adequate attention to the overall food situation, although it did try to control the price hike. A government order was issued in June 1942 legally fixing the maximum prices of coarse and medium rice in the Calcutta market. A portion of the previously saved stock of rice was moved to Calcutta and distributed through ration shops to the general public. Simultaneously, the government tried to curb the export of rice from Bengal. Such policies brought some relief but they were far from sufficient."

"When the government started to take corrective measures, one of its first decisions was to requisition all available stock in the city and re-distribute the food-grains through ration shops and approved markets. This in turn led to a procurement drive on a more extensive scale. But the results were far from satisfactory and ended in the abandonment of the procurement drive and a withdrawal of the limit on the price of paddy and rice. The volume of supplies to Calcutta increased but so did the price. Starvation and death continued unabated, with the highest death rate in December 1943.

"The British Army too tried to combat the spreading famine by providing food and organized nearly 11 crore free meals, an effort that proved to be too little too late. In fact, when the Secretary of State for India, Leo Amery, first requested England's Prime Minister Winston Churchill for releasing food stocks for India, Churchill responded with a telegram asking, 'If food is so scarce, why hasn't Gandhi died yet?'"

A twitter of laughter and disapproving sounds went around the class. Amartya paused to let the students digest the implication of the remark.

"Finally, with the arrival of supplies from other parts of India, the price and the intensity of the famine lessened but the death rate remained high throughout 1944 due to the outbreak of cholera, small pox and malaria. It was only by the end of 1945 and towards early 1946 that the hunger, poverty and disease caused by the famine began to reduce."

As the students bent their heads low to make notes in their books, Amartya paused and then said, "But that's one point of view. Want to hear mine?"

The students glanced up in surprise. There was more?

"Remember I said that these people may have died even if they'd had enough money to eat?"

"So are you saying there's another cause for the food shortage?"

"I'm saying that there was little food shortage to begin with. And I'm saying it wasn't the food shortage that was the primary cause of the famine."

Amartya received several surprised looks. This was the crux of his whole argument and he let his statement register before he continued.

"What I have attempted to do in my research is analyze famines as broad 'economic' problems of hunger and deprivation. In attempting to determine the cause of a famine, I evaluate it in terms of how people buy food or get entitled to it rather than in terms of the grossly undifferentiated picture of aggregate food supply for the economy as a whole."

"With regard to the Bengal famine, in particular, there's considerable evidence to suggest that the crop hadn't been bad in any sense, so it was surprising that there would be a famine. The Famine Inquiry Commission appointed by the Raj later reported that the food statistics must have been wrong. But in fact, when I studied it much later, it was clear that the food statistics weren't really very wrong."

"According to my analysis, the overall production of rice was within the normal range, taking into account the normal standard variation. In fact, the total rice production in the year 1943, which was 7.628 million tonnes, was more than in 1941, 6.768 million tonnes, prior to the famine. Thus, the famine had largely been man-made. It was not the shortage of rice production but its unavailability that had resulted in the skyrocketing of its price. The ongoing inflation aggravated the price hike further. Rumours of shortage due to war-time demands resulted in a price inflation. Although Bengal had enough rice and other grains to feed its people, millions had been left without purchasing power. Speculation, hoarding and profiteering were the main factors responsible for the spectacular rise in prices."

Amartya noticed how furiously the students were taking notes, some even involved in discussions of their own in the back rows. He didn't mind students talking in his classes. His idea was to intellectually stimulate them as best he could and allow them to discuss, debate, infer.

He continued, "The statistics needed only minor correction, and that wouldn't explain the famine. One must see it plainly in terms of a fuller economic analysis of how people earn a living and how they can use their wages and income to buy food. Just to give an example, sharecroppers and cash wage labourers in normal circumstances are almost equally poor, but the famine hit the wage labourers much harder than the sharecroppers. Here we come to what we've discussed so far. World War II. The Japanese are in Burma and the British army in Bengal. War-based production. Prices shoot up. When the prices shot up, the wage earners, with fixed money wages, started feeling the impact right away, whereas sharecroppers, since they get their income in the form of part of the food, didn't suffer in the same way. Indeed, I found on the basis of indicators of mortality as well as indicators of occupational distress on which we had data that sharecroppers were not distressed at all in the way that cash wage labourers were. This indicated that I was on the right line. So the kind of economic analysis, the complexity of the entire economic system could be brought into the story. This is a simple example; there were more complex issues as well, such as the effect of government procurement and of speculation by traders. Basically, the recognition that the story was not just about food was already clear when I watched the famine and its class-based nature, its suddenness and its contrariness."

"In other words, a famine is not caused by a negative Malthusian relationship between population and food supply but by the inability of famine-prone individuals to access food in times of great need, even when food supplies are adequate."

Continuing his lecture the next day, Amartya touched upon another aspect of famines that he had been researching—the relation between famines and government systems.

"You can't prevent under-nourishment so easily, but famines you can stop with half an effort, without difficulty."

"So why *don't* the governments stop them?" someone piped up.

"Well, the first answer is that the government servants and the leaders, whether they be military or non-military, are upper class. They never starve. They never suffer from famine, and therefore they don't have a personal incentive to stop it. However, if the government were vulnerable to public opinion, then famines are a dreadfully bad thing to have. You can't win many elections after a famine, and you don't like being criticized by newspapers, opposition parties in Parliament and so on if you are in a democratic country. Democracy gives the government an immediate political incentive to act."

"Prof, is that why you've written in your book that famines never occur in a democracy?"

"Never say never, but yes, that is my belief. It became increasingly clear to me by the 1970s that famines have actually not occurred in functioning democracies and also that that didn't seem like a fluke but there was a good reason. Given that political incentive, and taking note of the economic analysis that famines are easy to prevent, you would expect that in a democracy there will be no famine. Whereas in the absence of a democracy you may avoid famine if you are lucky. A famine may not develop. On the other hand, if one were to develop, there's no guarantee that the government will try to prevent it."

"But surely, Prof, sometimes there could be that one person who genuinely works for the people without thinking of the pay-back?"

"Of course, that possibility always exists, and it's what gives economists like me some hope… the hope that we'll be proven wrong," Amartya said with a smile. "Some time there will be a visionary leader who will actually do it without needing the political incentive, but you don't have the guaranteed reaction by the government which you would expect in a democracy. If there is no democracy there can be only a dictatorship, either of an alienated kind, like a colonial administration, like the British Raj in India or for that matter in Ireland, or military dictators in one country after another, like Somalia, Ethiopia and many other countries. Also, the one-party states like we had in the Soviet Union and China, despite the fact that the governments were generally committed to the interests of the underdog, indeed, that's how they had come to power, they were so dominated by theory that they were not in a position to react. Often they were particularly inhumane in not feeling the manifest suffering that they saw around them, thinking that somehow in the long run this would turn out to be right.

"Countries with dictatorial regimes like Sudan, Ethiopia, Somalia, Soviet Union, China and North Korea have experienced some of the worst famines in history. In India, too, famines occurred only during the British Raj, before it became a democracy. On the other hand, present-day Bangladesh, which was under military rule for a considerable period of time, has faced recurring threats of famine."

"What happened in China?"

"China faced a catastrophic famine between 1958 and 1961 when as many as 30 million people starved to death. This despite the fact that China was economically stronger than India and that Beijing had developed a system of food distribution, public health care and education at a much faster pace than India."

"So what went wrong?"

"The lack of a democracy, of course," Amartya said in a matter-of-fact tone.

Many of the students laughed at the one who had thought to ask a question that had such an obvious answer.

Coming to his defence, Amartya spoke above the murmurs and laughs, "No, no, there is a more specific reason! Now while tens of millions were dying every year, the disastrous policies of the government were not revised for three years. This would be unthinkable in a democracy. Similarly, while the famine was going on, they were also starving of information from the government. This is an additional factor, the informational connection as opposed to the political incentive connection. This is because each commune in China, each collective, obviously saw that they were not doing very well themselves but they read in the papers that everything was fine in the rest of the country. That's what censorship does. They all came to the conclusion respectively that they alone were failing. So rather than admitting failure, they cooked the numbers and reported higher food output than was true. When Beijing added these up at the height of the famine, they thought that they had a hundred million more metric tons of rice than they actually had. So the censorship of the press which often goes with lack of a democratic system had the effect not only of hoodwinking the public but ultimately hoodwinking the state."

"Didn't something similar happen in the Soviet Union as well?"

"That's right. They were partly deluded and partly

theoretically arrogant and overconfident of their policy. But in the case of the Ukraine and the Soviet famine, there was also a kind of dislike of one group, the Kulaks, so there was somewhat of a basic lack of sympathy for the rural areas. But on top of that, the lack of democracy, of political incentives that go with democracy and the lack of information added to the story. So I think the one-party state in the Soviet Union or China or Cambodia or North Korea or the military dictatorship as in many of the African countries or the colonial rule like in the British Empire and the French Empire bring out plentifully the penalty of political unfreedom, the lack of democracy."

•

From the mid-1980s, Amartya continued his analysis of famines with the support of the World Institute of Development Economics Research (WIDER), Helsinki, where he worked with old friends Lal Jayawardena, a colleague from Cambridge, who was the director of the organization, and Siddiq Osmani, an ex-student of his who was leading its hunger and deprivation programme. He also worked with Martha Nussbaum, a scholar of classical philosophy as well as contemporary ethics and literary studies, on the cultural side of the programme. He later collaborated with Nussbaum on a number of studies from 1987 to 1989 and a collection of essays entitled *Quality of Life,* which was published in 1993.

By the mid-1980s, Amartya was collaborating extensively with the Belgian economist Jean Drèze. In characteristic Amartya Sen style, he credits Drèze with helping him understand hunger and deprivation and enabling his recent work on development, done jointly with him. In fact, he half-seriously claims, "It is hard to beat an arrangement for joint work whereby Jean does most of the work whereas I get a lot of the credit!"

Amartya's work on famines was largely done while at Harvard, which gave him the space and resources to explore his academic interests fully. By the late '80s, he was settled at Harvard as professor of economics. There, he also had the chance to teach a subject he had once studied a long time ago but never pursued as anything but a personal interest—philosophy. His work in both fields benefited greatly from his association with eminent colleagues like John Rawls and Tim Scanlon, Ziv Griliches, Dale Jorgenson, Janos Kornai, Stephen Marglin and others. He organized joint courses with Robert Nozick and Eric Maskin, with John Rawls and Thomas Scanlon in philosophy and with Jerry Green, Stephen Marglin and David Bloom in economics.

He also began work on some new problems, including the characterization of rationality, the demands of objectivity and the relation between facts and values. He started taking an interest in health equity, in public health in particular, in close collaboration with Sudhir Anand. According to Amartya, "Harvard's ample strength in an immense variety of subjects gives one scope for much freedom in the choice of work and of colleagues to talk to."

He remains grateful to Harvard for all this as well as the high quality of its students, as Amartya has always used the classes he conducted to learn more about the subjects he taught. Through his own life, Amartya has constantly demonstrated how learning truly never ends.

Over the next few years, Amartya kept moving along

with his children from one American university to another, and these included Stanford, Berkeley, Yale, Princeton, Harvard, UCLA (University of California) and the University of Texas.

While his children were very young, Amartya mainly stayed in the USA, but when they were old enough to take care of themselves, he moved back to his alma mater, the familiar Trinity College at Cambridge, as Master of Trinity from 1998 to 2004. In January 2004, however, he returned to Harvard to work as a Lamont University professor and professor of economics and philosophy and as Senior Fellow.

Kabir and Indrani, his two children with Eva, whom he has brought up single-handedly, have done well for themselves too. Presently, Indrani is working as a journalist in New York while Kabir, who perhaps inherited more of his genes from Amita Sen than Amartya, teaches music at a school in Boston and has a rock band called Uncle Trouble.

Amartya has had to live with tremendous distances between himself and the people he loves but through it all he has cultivated a warm and supportive relationship with all his children. In 1991 he married Emma Rothschild, a Fellow at King's University, Cambridge, England and Director of the Centre for History and Economics. She teaches philosophy at Cambridge and, like Amartya, is a devoted academic and is considered to be an expert on the renowned Scottish philosopher and economist Adam Smith.. In Emma, Amartya has found a supportive partner in his work and personal life.

Whether a man is judged on his professional or his personal successes, Amartya stands tall on both counts—an accomplished academic and a much loved father and husband — all this despite the adversities life has thrown his way.

The ink of the scholar is more sacred than
the blood of the martyr

— *Prophet Mohammed* —

9

THE PRACTICAL ACADEMIC

"Mark Twain has described a cauliflower as 'nothing but cabbage with a college education'." The four hundred strong audience that had been waiting to listen to Amartya Sen's convocation address all morning burst into laughter. Amartya smiled his characteristic understated smile and looked down at the note cards placed before him.

It was the December of 2000. Amartya Sen, fresh from his Nobel Prize win, was touring the world receiving a slew of awards, honorary degrees and delivering lectures. From a Doctor of Letters at the University of Strathcylde in Scotland to a Laurea Honoris Causa at the University of Florence in Italy, Amartya has received close to fifty-three honorary degrees to date. Unlike most academics of his stature, he has always made it a point to personally receive all such honours. And of course when Amartya Sen is present in a room, he is rarely allowed to leave without delivering a speech. This habit earned Amartya the nickname Amartya 'Commencement' Sen!

Now at the Kerala University, which had just awarded him with an Honorary DLitt, Amartya was delivering a convocation speech on academia and its perceptions around the world.

"Many of the finest cauliflowers—from Shakespeare to Charles Dickens—overcame cabbageness without the benefit of college education. Yet there can be little doubt that good university education can make a dramatic difference to human abilities and achievements. Indeed, not only can it transform individual lives, its role in social change can be quite critical as well."

It would be natural for Amartya Sen to defend the academic way of life. He is after all a man who has spent most of his life living on campuses. He has never held a non-academic job, his present wife and both his ex-wives were academics, his children have been raised on university campuses around the world and he has always considered teaching to be the surest path to knowledge.

Amartya's reputation in academic circles is almost incomparable given his breadth of knowledge not just of economics but also of philosophy, history and culture. As a full-time or visiting professor at numerous prestigious universities both in India and around the world, Amartya Sen has spread his knowledge and wisdom amongst a large body of students fortunate enough to be taught by him and colleagues fortunate to have worked with him. As he jokingly says, "Between my four children, and the two of us, the universities that the Sen family has encountered include Calcutta University, Cambridge University, Jadavpur University, Delhi University, LSE, Oxford University, Harvard University, MIT, University of California, Stanford University, Cornell University, Smith College, Wesleyan University, among others. Perhaps one day we can jointly write an illustrated guide to the universities."

No matter where Amartya has lived or taught, his students and colleagues alike have usually been astounded by his extraordinary intellectual prowess. Robert Cassen, an economist at the London School of Economics, has commented, "He has a mind like a searchlight, yet he works at Mozartian speed. His output is staggering in its volume."

Often the word 'academic' has a negative connotation. As Amartya said in his address to the Kerala University, "It is typically not high praise to be told that one's argument is 'academic'. The dictionaries give the meaning of the word as 'theoretical' or 'conjectural' or 'unpractical'. All this is quite understandable. And yet the real world does need the theories, the conjectures, the unpractical demands, to reexamine what it has got and to decide where to go from there."

To many people, the word 'academic' can also suggest someone who is out of touch with reality and lives in an ivory tower. Says Amartya on this, "There is, of course, the possibility that the idea of a quiet education at a university may sound somewhat distant and even elitist. Indeed, the association of university education with elitism is common enough in many people's mind. Certainly, elitist pursuits can draw on university education, but the important point to note is that the purist of equality, justice and other radical concerns can also draw on the universities."

The unfortunate fact is that many academics in fact live up to (or down to) this reputation and often spend their lives hiding away from reality in the protected environs of college campuses.

Amartya has never been such an academic. He explains, "I am used to thinking of the word 'academic' as meaning 'sound', rather than the more old-fashioned dictionary meaning, 'unpractical', 'theoretical' or 'conjectural'." Although a majority of Amartya's life has been spent on campuses, he has also travelled into villages and towns, seeking to understand the depth of the human experience. To Amartya, economics has not just been a subject of academic interest but a means to understanding the nature of the world and the society we live in. He has approached economics as not just a subject to be studied but as a practical tool kit for changing lives and enabling people to have a richer, more fruitful existence.

To this end, he has made profound contributions in the field of welfare economics, including social choice theory, poverty and welfare indexes, distribution, the study of famines, individual welfare and collective decision making aimed at the general masses, especially the poor and the deprived class. He has devoted a large part of his career to solving issues for the betterment of poor. "He's very concerned about justice," says Sudhir Anand, Professor of Economics at Oxford. "Most of his work has been linked by his interest in the welfare of the most impoverished and monetarily deprived section of the society."

No wonder then that Amartya is often called 'the conscience of economics', for having humanized an academic field heretofore considered cold and disconnected from the day-to-day life of man.

•

So, now that the professor had achieved it all—fame, wealth, awards, and even the Nobel Prize—did he consider slowing down or retiring? Amartya Sen? Never. Just a couple of years later, Sen sat at his desk in his London home, putting the finishing touches to his new book, *The Argumentative Indian,* which would be published in 2005. Despite all of his academic commitments, Amartya found the time to produce a large body of work, publishing close to thirty books and a hundred articles. His first book, *Choice of Techniques*, dealing with the problem of the choice of the right techniques for maximizing production in an underdeveloped economy, was published in 1960 to positive reviews. His next book, *Collective Choice and Social Welfare,* paved the way in the field of welfare economics. In *The Argumentative Indian: Writings on Indian History, Culture and Identity,* Amartya presented a collection of sixteen essays, many of which were reworked lectures and previously published pieces, discussing the identity of contemporary India.

When Amartya Sen writes a book, it always gets noticed, and his books have often been reviewed in publications like *The Economist* and *The New York Times.* In a glowing review in *The Guardian,* reviewer Soumya Bhattacharya describes the book in these words: "One of the book's many triumphs is its tone. Sen does not indulge in triumphalism about his country's past; nor does he spare Western influences (like James Mill's History of British India) that have oversimplified and distorted the Indian reality... This is a book that needed to have been written. The perception of India in the West and, indeed, among Indians themselves has never been more amorphous as it is now. *The Argumentative Indian* will provide a new dimension and perspective to that perception. It would be no surprise if it were to become as defining and as influential a work as Edward Said's *Orientalism.*"

One of his most reviewed and most popular books is *The Idea of Justice* in which he presented an alternative to the prevailing faulty justice system, in a direct challenge to well-known political philosopher John Rawls.

Apart from the Nobel Prize (also known as the Sveriges Riksbank Prize in Economic Science), Amartya has been awarded numerous other prizes for his work. He has received several awards from Trinity College, Cambridge, and the Indira Gandhi Gold Medal Award of the Asiatic Society in 1994. In 1999, one year after his Nobel win, he was awarded the Bharat Ratna, the highest civilian award in India for the "recognition of public service of the highest order". In 2003, the Lifetime Achievement Award was conferred upon Amartya by the Indian Chamber of Commerce, and he also received the Lifetime Achievement Award from the Bangkok-based United Nations Economic and Social Commission for Asia and the Pacific (UNESCAP). More recently, he received the International Humanist Award from the International Humanist and Ethical Union (IHEU) in 2002. That same year, he was also awarded the Eisenhower Medal and the Leontief Prize for his contributions in the field of economics from the Global Development and Environment Institute (GDAE), Tuft's

University, Boston.

Amartya was elected as president of the American Economic Association in 1993 and also served as president of the Econometric Society in 1984, the International Economic Association from 1986 to 1989, the Indian Economic Association in 1989 and the American Economic Association in 1994. He is a Fellow of the British Academy, the Econometric Society and an honorary Fellow of Trinity College, Cambridge. He is also a foreign honorary member of the American Academy of Arts and Sciences and of the American Philosophical Association.

Prior to this, in 1997, he received the Edinburgh Medal and the Mahalanobis Prize in 1976. He was also honoured with the Frank E. Seidman Distinguished Award in political economy (1986), the Senator Giovanni Agnelli International Prize in Ethics (1990), the Alan Shawn Feinstein World Hunger Award (1990), the Jean Mayer Global Citizenship Award 1993 and the Catalonia International Prize (1997).

In May 2007, Amartya was appointed Chairman of the Nalanda Mentor Group to direct the Nalanda University Project, which seeks to elevate the Nalanda University, Bihar, to international status. Nalanda is where students and scholars from countries like Korea, Japan, China, Tibet, Indonesia, Persia and Turkey came to study until AD 1197. Who could be a better choice than Amartya Sen to take this ancient institution back to its past glory?

But Amartya's greatest achievement is perhaps the sheer drive and motivation that he brings to each day of his life. Even after achieving more than most of his colleagues, more than most expected from him, he has always found a new challenge, a new horizon. He is unmatched in his thirst for knowledge. He is the eternal student who pushes himself to learn more with each day, to improve himself with each step. Close friend Sunil Sengupta recalls how Amartya's wife Eva had once jokingly complained about Amartya working eighteen hours a day. Sengupta had then considered this an exaggeration, but on a visit to their house in London, he happened to wake early one morning to find Amartya hard at work while his family was in deep slumber.

Amartya's achievements have not come to him easily. His empirical work has occasionally been criticized for not being original or for lacking detail and depth. Alex de Waal, author of *Famine Crimes*, a book about how democracy prevents famines, countered Amartya's opinion saying that the presence of a democratic government is not enough to prevent famine. He claims that the main cause of famine is an epidemic rather than starvation and has criticized Amartya's work on this subject. Others have said that it has been relatively easy for him to win the Nobel Prize as he spent most of his life outside India, in comparison to other Indians who have won the Nobel Prize while working within their country with not as many facilities. Robert L. Pollock wrote in the *Wall Street Journal* that Amartya's work was remarkable "only for the extent to which his renown outstripped the quality of his work." In another article entitled "The Wrong Economist Won", he wrote that if the prize had to be for development economics, it should have gone to Peter Bauer, who he believed was a better candidate than Amartya. According to him, Bauer has consistently fought the "misguided belief" that government aid promotes economic growth.

All of this criticism has never fazed Amartya who has steadily moved on to becoming one of the world's greatest authorities on welfare economics and famine prevention. He has received numerous offers from the Indian government as well as governments of various other countries to work as their advisor. However, he has always turned down offers that would take away his independence. In January 2008, President of France Nicolas Sarkozy announced that Amartya Sen along with American Nobel Laureate Joseph Stiglitz would advise the French government on economic growth. Sarkozy is said to have been greatly influenced by the United Nations Human Development Index developed by Sen along with Mahbub-ul-Haq. Despite this worldwide demand, Amartya's heart remains in India and he takes pride in maintaining his Indian citizenship and his simple Indian lifestyle.

With such a long roster of achievements, and many more to come, the question begs to be asked—what drives Amartya Sen? What fuels his concerns for the world he lives in? What pushes him to ask tough questions and seek their answers? Answering these questions in a 2001 interview, Amartya described his motivations and compulsions in the following words, "If one thinks about the people who live in a world in which they need not be hungry, in which they need not die without medical care, in which they need not be illiterate, they need not feel hopeless and miserable so much of the time, and yet they are, that seems to be scandalous… Since we live in a global village, events in different parts of the world influence each other. The Internet begins to penetrate in my country. Indians begin to find out how other people live in the rest of the world. Given these circumstances, the issues of inequality and the issue of poverty are not separable even globally. They're very closely linked, both in terms of the need to ask the moral question, is it right that I should enjoy my privileges, and not feel I owe anything to others? As well as the other level, do I have a right to be content living in a world with so much poverty and inequality? Both these questions motivate us to take these issues to be central to human living."

Perhaps there is no greater argument for academia than Amartya Sen's life and the constant intellectual stimulation, drive and inspiration he has found through the campus life. As Amartya says, "University campuses [are not] quite as far removed from life as is often presumed. Robert Goheen has remarked, 'If you feel that you have both feet planted on level ground, then the university has failed you.' Right on. But then who wants to be planted on ground? There are places to go."

To me, it seems a dreadful indignity to have a soul controlled by geography

— *George Santayana* —

10

THE GLOBAL INDIAN

It was a bright spring morning in Calcutta in 1984, the year Amartya Sen and friend Sunil Sengupta travelled into the villages of West Bengal to study gender inequality in India. Taking a rare break from their work, the pair of researchers had arrived in Calcutta and were en route to visit their alma mater, Santiniketan.

Sitting in the back seat of the grey Ambassador that was speeding along scenic streets towards Santiniketan, the two were looking forward to seeing their old school after many years. When the driver needed a break, they parked to have a cup of tea at a roadside stall. Strolling back to the car, sipping tea, Sengupta turned to his friend, "So Amartya... you think this is the year for the Nobel?"

Sengupta had casually mentioned something that had been a sore point for almost everyone he knew—everyone but Amartya. Amartya's family and colleagues had long believed that the professor was worthy of receiving the Nobel Prize for economics, but year after year, he had been nominated and then rejected. Some were beginning to feel it was a case of discrimination. But not Amartya. He smiled and continued to sip his tea in silence. After a minute, Amartya spoke, but it was to change the topic. "How's the family, Sunil? We've been so busy with work, I haven't even had time to come meet them."

"They're good... all well. My sister's brother-in-law was asking for my opinion just yesterday on whether he should go abroad for higher studies. I wasn't sure what to say to him."

Amartya retorted, "Why not? Why shouldn't he go?"

"Well..." Sengupta began to speak, then decided against it. His opinions on going abroad differed from Amartya's. At the same time, he understood Amartya well. He realized that Amartya did not harbour any aversion for India; he was simply open to the idea of going abroad for professional or educational reasons, as he believed having a global vision was important for personal growth. This was one of the things he had learned at Santiniketan and it was what had exposed him to new ideas and ways of thinking, which in turn had helped develop his own work.

Sengupta was also aware that Amartya was a man who had a house in many places but whose home would always be India. He knew how much Amartya loved and respected his country and that he did not have to reside in it to prove it. In Amartya's heart, the word 'home' would always be associated with India and, in particular, with Santiniketan. No wonder that, to date, he has retained his Indian citizenship, though he could have relinquished it for a more coveted American or British passport decades ago.

Sengupta remembered one afternoon at Santiniketan when he had gone to visit Amartya's mother, Amita Sen. The television was on and Amita had been carefully watching an interview of Amartya when Sengupta walked in.

"Another interview...?" he asked in Bengali, flopping down on the sofa next to Amita's chair.

"Look at this, Sunil..." Amita replied, a small frown on her face.

"What is it? What's wrong?"

"They're asking Babloo about the greatest influences in his life, and he hasn't mentioned Santiniketan once!"

Sengupta smiled. He knew Amartya well. Santiniketan was intrinsic to Amartya Sen. If he had not mentioned it, it was probably because it just seemed too ingrained, too obvious.

"Don't worry, Ma..." Sunil said. A childhood friend of Amartya's, Amita was a maternal figure for Sunil too. In turn, in Sunil, Amita had found a son and enjoyed the time he would spend at *Pratichi,* her house in Santiniketan, especially since Amartya had gone abroad.

"You know how much Amartya loves Santiniketan. It's the first place he comes to when he visits India! And he does that once a year! That's a lot more than most people who settle abroad."

Amita nodded along, still appearing decidedly unhappy.

Trying to lift her spirits, Sunil tried to change the subject.

"Hey, Ma, remember last year when he had come down for the *Poush Mela* with Emma?"

The memory instantly brought a smile to Amita's face.

One of Amartya's favourite events to attend in India was the *Poush Mela* or the Monsoon Fair that was held annually at Santiniketan. The festival, which had been started by the founder of Santiniketan, Rabindranath Tagore, features live performances of Bengali folk music, especially Baul music. It also marks the Foundation Day of Santiniketan and features a bustling market full of local craftspersons selling traditional handicrafts and traditional performances.

"Oh he was so eager to take Emma around and show her all the performances. When they came back, she told me, 'I feel like I have lived a part of Amartya's childhood today'," said Amita. "I can't wait till they come back again. He must be missing his *dudh, muri aur kola.*" A Bengali delicacy of milk, puffed rice and bananas, it was a favourite of Amartya's.

Amita Sen's son has often been accused of 'abandoning' the country where he received the education that has made him who he is today, but those who adopt this line of argument seem to give no heed to the hard work he has since put in to achieve what he has. They are also blind to Amartya's love for his country as well as the work he does for it—work that he makes no effort to tout or promote in the press.

When in Santiniketan, the Nobel Laureate wanders around the Visva-Bharati campus on bicycle, making it a point to visit the Subarnarekha bookshop and have a cup of *chai* at the tea stall, *Kalor Dokan.* Says Indranath Mazumdar, owner of Subarnarekha, "Amartya always looks up his old friends who still live here. Clad in kurta-pyjama, he stands in the queue to buy a railway ticket from Santiniketan to Calcutta, and no one would guess that he is a Professor at Harvard and Cambridge."

In 1983, Amartya repaid his school for all its contributions to his life in the best way he could—during a professional visit to Calcutta to research gender inequality in India, he served as visiting faculty at Visva-Bharati for the duration of the year. He also maintains regular contact with universities and schools where he has previously taught, especially the Delhi School of Economics. Amartya explains, "While I have worked abroad since 1971, I have constantly retained close connections with Indian universities, I have, of course, a special relation with Delhi University, where I have been an honorary professor since leaving my full-time job there in 1971, and I use this excuse to subject Delhi students to lectures whenever I get a chance. For various reasons—personal as well as academic—the peripatetic life seems to suit me, in this respect. After my student days in Cambridge in 1953–56, I guess I have never been away from India for more than six months at a time. This—combined with my remaining exclusively an Indian citizen—gives me, I think, some entitlement to speak on Indian public affairs, and this remains a constant involvement."

These 'personal' reasons Amartya speaks of when explaining his nomadic lifestyle are primarily related to the continuing treatment he needs following his brush with mouth cancer as a student. He however ensures that he visits India at every possible opportunity. He remains closely involved with Indian public affairs and openly expresses his views about them. In doing so, he has been sharply critical of the Indian government for not working hard enough to eliminate illiteracy or mass poverty among its citizens. These admonitions are usually paid serious heed to, since they are based on sound economic theory and are not simply the uncorroborated opinions of a politically inclined Leftist academic.

Another part of India Amartya often visits aside from Santiniketan and Calcutta is Bangladesh in whose capital city of Dhaka he spent his childhood. Not only does he have ancestral roots in Bangladesh, some of his closest friends and collaborators live there as well, including Rehman Sobhan, Anisur Rehman and Kamal Hossain.

The greatest proof of Amartya's commitment to his country, however, lies in how he used his Nobel Prize award money. In a brief autobiography he penned for the Nobel Prize committee, Amartya spoke of this: "When the Nobel award came my way, it also gave me an opportunity to do something immediate and practical about my old obsessions, including literacy, basic health care and gender equity, aimed specifically at India and Bangladesh. The *Pratichi Trust*, which I have set up with the help of some of the prize money, is, of course, a small effort compared with the magnitude of these problems. But it is nice to re-experience something of the old excitement of running evening schools, more than fifty years ago, in villages near Santiniketan."

Set up in 1999, today, the *Pratichi Trust,* named after his home in Santiniketan, is dedicated to solving the problems bothering Amartya since his early student days—literacy, basic health care and gender equality in India and Bangladesh.

Even when not in the country, Amartya remains one of its most credible ambassadors. He has often been the voice of reason that has defended India against accusations and misunderstandings. At the Sixteenth Morgenthau Memorial Lecture on Ethics & Foreign Policy at New York in 1997, for instance, Amartya countered the argument that Asian values do not give freedom the same importance as the values propounded in Western nations. Staunchly defending Asia, and with it India, Amartya demonstrated the importance attached to freedom in Asian countries. While some Americans believe that terms like 'political freedom', 'civil liberties' and 'democracy' are purely Western ideals, Amartya stated that it was wrong to think of political tolerance as a 'Western liberal inclination' simply because freedom and democracy have been seriously violated there. As a supporter of the democratic system throughout his life, he emphasized the importance of a democratic government in achieving the economic growth of the masses, all the while showing how India is one of the world's newest and most successful democracies. Apart from India, he also made references to other Asian countries like Singapore, China and Japan as well as to religions like Islam, Buddhism, Hinduism and Confucianism to show that the concept of tolerance is deeply embedded in Asian culture since historic times. At the same time, he has supported globalization, which he feels contributes to prosperity and human development, but only if backed by adequate national policies in a conducive social and economic environment, that is, an environment wherein greater attention is paid to education, health care and land reforms.

Due to the cultural diversity in the Asian subcontinent, there tends to be a corresponding variety of views on freedom, tolerance and equality. Amartya pointed towards the diversity in the Asian value system as seen in the principles of the Buddhist tradition and the theories of Confucius, which clearly states that the two main pillars of Asian values are loyalty and sincerity to one's family and country.

He went on to discuss how tolerance has been emphasized by Indian rulers since ancient times. Emperor Asoka supported equality at the very fundamental level and demonstrated this through his edicts. The Mughal Emperor Akbar too abolished *jaziya*—tax on religious pilgrimages—to demonstrate his belief in impartiality.

In his book, *The Argumentative Indian,* Amartya has also spoken out against the West's typically skewed perception of India that according to him tends to be 'exoticist' and 'curatorial', placing far too much emphasis on India's religiosity. In a scathing attack on such views, Amartya has presented examples from India's history of its rationalist, scientific, mathematical and secular heritage, fields treated by Orientalists as 'Western spheres of success'.

Perhaps Shashi Tharoor, writer and Member of Parliament, who reviewed this book for *The Washington Post* sums up both the book as well as Amartya's place in the world with the following words: "Sen is a cosmopolitan and an Indian—and he, of course, would see no contradiction in those terms. Educated at Rabindranath Tagore's experimental school, Santiniketan (where the earlier Bengali Nobelist prophetically dubbed Sen 'Amartya', or 'immortal'), and at Cambridge University, the first non-English Master of Trinity College, Cambridge, the holder of two named professorships at Harvard, film buff, cricket fan and voracious reader, Sen embodies the yearning for heterodox learning."

There is one great society alone on the earth:
the noble living and the noble dead

— *Wordsworth* —

11

GETTING THE NEWS

Amita Sen sat on a cane chair, fanning herself with a newspaper. The electricity had gone again and although it was October, the late afternoon sun was pouring in through her windows and it was warm without the ceiling fan.

Now eighty-seven, much of Amita's day was spent sitting in that chair in her living room at *Pratichi*, her home in Santiniketan, lovingly gazing at the many framed pictures hanging on the walls around her. Some were portraits of family members, some watercolours but most were photographs of her son, Babloo, standing next to important people, receiving awards, delivering speeches.

Babloo called every alternate day and she had spoken to him just that morning at precisely 8 am, his usual time. He had told her he was in New York for the day and described to her how festive the city looked from his hotel room window. She loved hearing the little details of his surroundings and his work—it made her feel closer to him.

The large clock resting on the table behind Amita's chair had just ticked to 3 pm when her phone rang. Startled, she reached for it, wondering who it could be. Her daily routine was fairly fixed and she wasn't used to phone calls at this time of day. At once, her mind jumped to last week when just such an untimely phone call had brought the news that her brother-in-law had passed away. With a trembling hand, she picked up the receiver.

"Hello…?" she said in a slightly shaky voice.

"Ma, this is Babloo. Were you resting? Am I disturbing you?"

Babloo? Again?

Worried, she asked, "Is everything all right? Are you okay?"

"Yes, Ma, I'm fine. Just a bit cold. It's getting quite chilly here; how is it there?" Amartya asked with a smile in his voice. He knew she was bursting to know why he'd called.

"Oh, the electricity has gone again so it's quite hot here… But forget all that. Why have you called again? You just called this morning!"

Realizing his mother was more worried than curious, Amartya didn't make her wait any longer. Casually he said,

"Ma, I wanted you to be the first to know... I think this time they have given me the award."

He did not have to mention which award he was referring to.

He heard an exclamation at the other end of the line and then a laugh. His mother was obviously having trouble using words to express her happiness. Amartya laughed as well, and mother and son spent a few minutes catching their breath. After a pause, what his mother said next came as no surprise to Amartya. He had guessed what she had been thinking.

"I wish your father were alive... he really believed it would happen one day..."

"I know, Ma, I wish he were here too."

Amartya's father had passed away in 1971, by which time Amartya had been nominated and rejected for the prize several times. Ashutosh Sen had not lived to see his dream becoming a reality, and it was a bittersweet moment for both Amartya and his mother.

Just the previous year, in 1997, an online poll of economists around the world had shown Dr Amartya Sen to be the most preferred candidate to win the 1998 Nobel Prize in economics. He had won the poll, receiving 76 votes while the other contender, MIT economist Paul Krugman, was given only 10 votes. A campaign headed by Kenneth Arrow, who himself had won the Nobel Prize for economics in 1972 for his pioneering contributions to the theory of social choice and the impossibility theorem, was launched by *The Times* in London to build pressure on the Nobel Prize committee to award the prize to Amartya Sen. Whether the committee recognized it or not, economists knew that he had long deserved the prize. These efforts finally bore fruit in 1998.

In a choked voice overwhelmed with joy, Amita said, "But Babloo, I won't believe it until I see it in print! I'm not going to discuss this with anyone until I see it in the newspapers tomorrow."

She heard her son laugh on the phone as he said, "Ma, this time the news is real."

Amita laughed along with her son, simultaneously wiping away tears from her eyes.

Amita did not have to wait for the papers the next day. In less than a day, the news had travelled and her house was filled with journalists interviewing her about her son and trying to get a glimpse of the woman who had given birth to the brilliant economist. Soon after, Amartya was on every television channel, being interviewed about his win.

Amartya's reaction to the sudden media attention was typically measured. On being interviewed in Manhattan the next morning, he described his response to the phone call from the Nobel committee with the words, "I was surprised and quite pleased when I got a call from the Royal Academy. I was even more pleased when they told me that the prize was for my work in welfare economics. I am thrilled because the subject, welfare economics, which I have worked on, did deserve more recognition, since it touches the lives of ordinary people. However, many economists have worked on the subject and it is a tragedy we can't all share the award." In typical Amartya Sen fashion, he had moved the attention away from himself to his work, whose credit he chose to share with others even in his moment of glory. He also said that after receiving the phone call at 5 am, the first thing he needed was a cup of coffee!

Back in India, Amartya's countrymen were ecstatic at the news. He received congratulatory messages from both the then Prime Minister Atal Behari Vajpayee and President KR Narayanan who described it as a "well-merited honour". Finance Minister Yashwant Sinha too congratulated Amartya and hailed his contribution to welfare economics and his work on poverty and famines. Dr Arjun Sengupta, former member of the Planning Commission, perhaps summed up everyone's thoughts best when he said, "Dr Sen is the most deserving candidate who should have got the award long back. He is a genius whose total span of scholarship and inspiring leadership covers not only philosophy, art, culture but has produced a generation of students both in India and the West... I am sure quite a few of them would get the Nobel Prize in the future."

It was the Indian community of economists and social scientists however who were most thrilled at the news. Economists nationwide praised Amartya for his achievement, and his colleagues at Trinity College were especially jubilant. In a message sent by the Delhi School of Economics where Amartya taught for eight years until 1971, his colleagues expressed their profound joy, saying that the prize was "rightly deserved and long overdue". "He is an excellent conservationist and absolutely brilliant," said Prof Badal Mukherjee, Director of the Delhi School of Economics. On his subsequent visit to Delhi, the Delhi School of Economics presented him with an honorary doctorate of letters. In his acceptance address, Amartya spoke in glowing terms about his experience at D School. "It all began here in lectures," he said. "Social theory and welfare economics emerged during question and answer sessions at Delhi." The prolific author also quipped that Delhi had taught him "never to publish a book unless you have tried it out on your students."

There was no limit to the extent of joy experienced by the general Indian population. As news of his receiving the Nobel Prize spread through the city of Calcutta, a wave of jubilation ran through the Bengali population, especially among the residents of Santiniketan. A son of their soil had been given the highest recognition in his field.

As one lamp lights another, nor grows less,
so nobleness enkindleth nobleness

— *James Russell Lowell* —

12

THE NOBEL PRIZE

What is it about the Nobel Prize that makes it more important than all the other awards and honours Amartya has received?

To answer this question, we must go back in time to the year 1888. Imagine this. Alfred Bernhard Nobel is sitting in a hotel room in Cannes, France. He is here to bury his brother, Ludwig, who has died while visiting the French city, far from his home in Sweden. Alfred is distraught but pragmatic. He knows that life must continue. He has faced death before; he knows how to move on. Alfred idly picks up the day's newspaper to distract himself. Scanning the headlines, he comes across an article that is an obituary. *His* obituary.

The headline reads, "*Le marchand de la mort est mort.*" He is fluent in French. The French newspaper has mistaken him for his brother. And the headline reads, "The merchant of death is dead."

How does it feel to read that about oneself? What does it prompt a man to do when he finds people are relieved at the thought of his death? But first, why was Alfred considered 'the merchant of death'?

Born on October 21, 1833, Alfred was the son of Immanuel Nobel, a Swedish engineer and inventor who made a fortune in the construction business and by providing equipment to the Russian army. Immanuel's invention of submerged wooden casks full of gunpowder deterred the British Royal Navy from moving within firing range of St. Petersburg during the Crimean War (1853–1856). With this success, Immanuel soon became a pioneer in the manufacture of arms.

The business of war was a profitable one, and Immanuel was able to give his four sons a superior home education, hiring university-level professors. By the age of seventeen, therefore, Alfred had received sound training in the natural sciences, literature and languages. In fact, he was fluent in five languages, developed a deep interest in chemistry and often wrote short pieces of fiction.

In Paris to study chemical engineering, Alfred happened to meet the young Italian chemist Ascanio Sobrero who had recently invented nitroglycerine, a highly explosive liquid. The liquid was on its own too explosive and dangerous to be put to any practical use, but Alfred immediately recognized its potential use in construction. Back in Sweden in 1852,

Alfred worked on developing commercial uses for nitroglycerine.

Alfred's work was misunderstood to begin with. Unlike him, others did not see nitroglycerine as something that could help people or be used commercially. One of his experiments caused an explosion that even killed his own brother Emil along with several others. That was when the authorities banned Alfred from continuing his work within Stockholm city limits. He responded, in his characteristic dogged style, by working on a barge anchored near Lake Mälaren.

Undeterred by his brother's death, Alfred continued with his work and soon had a breakthrough when he found that mixing nitroglycerine with *kieselguhr* would turn the liquid into a paste that could be shaped into rods of a size and form suitable for insertion into drilling holes. In 1867, he patented this product and called it 'dynamite', from the Greek 'dynamis', meaning power, a product that revolutionized construction.

Over the course of his life, Alfred Nobel became a successful businessman with factories and homes in more than twenty countries. Along with the mass production of dynamite, he kept experimenting with explosive technology and registered more than 300 patents.

If one focuses only on Alfred's work, he comes across as a one-dimensional, workaholic, cold-blooded businessman, albeit a technical genius and deeply intelligent. What can get ignored are other aspects of Alfred's personality—his three failed relationships that left him heartbroken and despondent, the poetry and short stories he wrote in his spare time and his deep interest in philosophy. From the journals he left behind, it is also clear he considered himself a hermit, a loner, who had never married and felt uncomfortable around people. For instance, one excerpt from his journals reads, "I am a misanthrope and yet utterly benevolent, have more than one screw loose yet am a super-idealist who digests philosophy more efficiently than food."

Looking upon Alfred in this way, we can begin to understand the impact the French newspaper headline must have had on him and how he must have felt reading the obituary that said, "Dr. Alfred Nobel, who became rich by finding ways to kill more people faster than ever before, died yesterday." Alfred had never worked with explosives with the intention of harming people, although harm had been done along the way, and it is then that he began to think about his legacy. In 1895, he signed his final will, and when it was discovered after his death in 1896, people were shocked by its contents. Alfred had decided to leave behind the majority of his fortune (approximately 31 million Swedish *kronor*) for the endowment of "prizes to those who, during the preceding year, shall have conferred the greatest benefit to mankind." And that is how the Nobel Prize came to be. By the morbid error that caused one man to introspect and choose to leave behind a better legacy after his death.

The Nobel Prize was initially awarded for physics, chemistry, physiology or medicine, literature and peace by the Nobel Foundation. It was only in 1968 that the Sveriges Riksbank Prize in Economic Sciences in the memory of Alfred Nobel was instituted by Sweden's Sveriges Riksbank, and the prize was first awarded in 1969. Even though the Sveriges Riksbank Prize in economics was not designated by Alfred

Nobel, its nomination process, selection criteria and presentation ceremony are similar to the Nobel Prize awarded in the other disciplines.

The Nobel Prize in the five core disciplines is awarded on December 10, Alfred Nobel's death anniversary, at the Stockholm Concert Hall in Sweden. The Nobel Peace Prize is also presented on the same date but at a separate ceremony held in Oslo, Norway. The prize is presented by King Carl XVI Gustaf of Sweden at a glittering ceremony in Stockholm and consists of a medal, a diploma and a cash award of approximately one million dollars. The medal is made of 18 carat gold and plated with 24 carat gold and bears Alfred Nobel's bust.

In his testament, Alfred Nobel had also mentioned the institutions that would be responsible for awarding the prizes. He designated The Royal Swedish Academy of Sciences for awarding the Nobel Prize in physics and chemistry, the Karolinska Institute for the Nobel Prize in physiology or medicine, the Swedish Academy for the Nobel Prize in literature and a committee of five persons belonging to the Norwegian Nobel Committee to be elected by the Norwegian Parliament (Storting) for deciding the recipient of the Nobel Peace Prize. When the Sveriges Riksbank Prize in Economics was instituted in the year 1968, the Royal Swedish Academy of Sciences was assigned the task of selecting the laureate in economics.

Each year, the respective Nobel Prize committees send individual invitations to thousands of members of academies, university professors, scientists, past Nobel laureates, members of parliamentary assemblies and others to submit the names of their candidates for the Nobel Prize for the coming year. The nominations are expected to reach the selection committee by January 31. Self-nominations are not accepted by the committee as are posthumous nominations, unless the deceased passed away after being nominated. The names that are nominated are not disclosed publicly, though the more popular ones do find their way to the media, as in the case of Amartya Sen about whom the press had been speculating a win for several years. After receiving the list of nominations, the Nobel Selection Committee selects the names of eminent personalities they feel should be considered for the Nobel Prize. They do not, of course, distinguish on the basis of nationality and in fact make every effort to best represent a wide cross section of achievers. The selected entries are then returned to the individual institutions by September or October.

What it means to even be short-listed for the Nobel, let alone receive it, can be garnered from the fact that of the thousand or so nominations received, only about 200 or 250 are short-listed. Furthermore, the committee even reserves the right to give no prize in a particular year if it finds no worthy candidate (and the prize can even be shared by two or three people). From the short-listed candidates, one is selected through the voting system by the prize-distributing institutions before the final selections are made by October 15. The various selection committees and institutions responsible for awarding the prize officially finally announce the names of the laureates who will receive the prize at the December ceremony. Immediately after the vote and selection of the final candidate, a press conference is held by the Nobel Prize-awarding institution in which the names are publicly announced for that particular year in each subject. The award decisions are final and cannot be appealed.

This elaborate and rigorous procedure for selecting a candidate was devised by Alfred Nobel himself, with the aim of creating a foolproof process for selecting the most worthy recipient.

Even still, the Prize has been dogged by its fair share of criticism and controversy. Alfred Nobel's great grand nephew Peter Nobel opposed the economics prize, arguing that it does not belong to any of the six categories as originally designated by Nobel. This has not prevented it from still being considered one of the greatest honours for an economist.

One of the greatest criticisms against the Nobel committee concerns another Indian, Mahatma Gandhi, who shockingly enough did not receive the Nobel Peace Prize. Gandhi, it is believed, passed away days before the closing date for the nominations in 1948 and the committee chose to not award the prize that year rather than award him posthumously.

The youngest person to win the Nobel Prize was William Laurence Bragg who was twenty-five when he received the prize for physics in 1915. The oldest Nobel laureate was Leoned Hurwicz who was awarded the prize in the year 2007 when he was 90 years old. Madam Curie was the first woman to receive the Nobel Prize and she received it twice, once in 1903 for physics and again in 1911 for chemistry. The Curie family perhaps has the highest number of Nobel Prizes in one family—Marie Curie won twice while her husband Pierre

Curie, their daughter Irene Joliot Curie and their son-in-law Fredric Joliot won once each.

The first prize in economics was awarded to Ragnar Frisch and Jan Tinbergen in 1969, while the first woman to receive a Nobel for economics is American economist Elinor Ostrom who shared the prize in 2009 with fellow American Oliver E. Williamson. Amartya Sen was the sixth Indian to receive the Nobel Prize. Other Indian Nobel laureates prior to Amartya Sen were Rabindranath Tagore for literature in 1913, Prof. C. V. Raman for physics in 1930, Prof. S. Chandrasekhar for physics in 1983, Dr. Hargobind Khurana for medicine in 1968 and Mother Teresa for peace in 1979. Indians to win the Nobel Prize after Amartya include V.S. Naipaul for literature in 2001, Rajendra Pachauri for peace in 2007 and Venkatraman Ramakrishnan for chemistry in 2009.

Two other institutions associated with the Nobel Prize are the Nobel Museum and the Nobel Library. The Nobel Museum at Stockholm was inaugurated in 2001 to celebrate the first century of the Nobel Prize since its inception in 1901. It was established in the fond memory of its founder, Alfred Nobel, as well as to remember Nobel laureates in their respective fields of excellence. The museum organizes exhibitions, films, plays and debates and has a bookshop, a souvenir shop and numerous cafes. The exhibits at the museum feature memorabilia from both celebrities and past laureates like Marie Curie, Nelson Mandela and Winston Churchill. Amartya has donated two of his favourite things to the museum—his childhood bicycle and a book on mathematics by Aryabhatta.

The Nobel Library of the Swedish Academy was founded on November 16, 1901, at Stockholm, to assist in the evaluation of the work done by the Nobel laureates. This is primarily done by acquiring the literary works and journals belonging to the laureates in their original languages for evaluation by the Swedish committee. In 2007, the library had a collection of about 2,00,000 volumes and is one of the largest libraries in northern Europe. The library also loans books to the general public and conducts lectures, seminars and symposia.

The history of the Nobel Prize is thus as colourful as it is distinguished and shows why receiving the award is a matter of such significance. The Nobel does not only represent the meaningfulness and importance of its winners' work but also their steadfast spirit, passion to improve this world we live in and their determination to carry on in the face of obstacles—qualities that the founder of the prize, Alfred Nobel, himself amply possessed.

No nobler feeling than this of
admiration for one higher than himself
dwells in the breast of man

— *Thomas Carlyle* —

13

D-DAY

It was December 10, 1998. The Concert Hall in Stockholm, Sweden, wore a bridal look. Flowers lined the famous wooden columns, and the audience, immaculately dressed in gowns and tails, added to the beauty of the hall. It was the moment of Dr. Amartya Sen's glory.

Dressed in a black suit and white bow tie, he stood with his head slightly bowed, evidently humbled, as Professor Robert Erikson of the Royal Academy of Sciences, delivered his presentation speech. Speaking of his contribution to social choice, Professor Erikson said, "Amartya Sen opened up a new field within the theory of social choice when he demonstrated how the possibility of identifying consistent social preferences is affected by the assumptions we make about the kinds of interpersonal comparison that can be made." He then spoke at length about his work on poverty and famines and how he succeeded in constructing measures to analyze welfare and develop famine-control mechanisms. Ending with a personal message to Amartya Sen, he said, "You have applied a consistent approach in your studies of social choice, welfare measurement, and poverty. In theoretical and empirical work, you have deepened the understanding of these issues, making fundamental contributions to welfare economics. It is a great honour and privilege for me to convey to you, on behalf of the Royal Swedish Academy of Sciences, our warmest congratulations. I now ask you to receive the Prize from His Majesty the King."

Amartya, more at home in a classroom than a banquet hall, walked uncertainly towards King Carl XVI Gustaf of Sweden who strode up to him and handed him the medal and diploma. It was at that moment that Amartya's face finally broke into a smile. As he shook hands with the King of Sweden, the glow on his face reflected the pride and joy he felt at being able to represent his country at this forum.

As is tradition, a few days prior to the ceremony, Amartya, like all of the other Nobel Laureates, had delivered a lecture on his life and his work. Besides the lecture, the laureates also attended numerous seminars and meetings with their colleagues along with visiting schools and universities so as to give a new generation of students the opportunity to interact with them.

The prize distribution ceremony was followed by a banquet at the Stockholm City Hall, attended by various past and current Nobel Laureates along with other distinguished guests. Among the illustrious gathering, Amartya truly was a first among equals.

On being asked what he would do with the prize money, Amartya said he hoped to spend a portion of the Nobel Prize money that won't be paid in taxes "on something good". True to his word, he later used the prize money to set up the *Pratichi Trust* to fund the education of girls in West Bengal and Bangladesh.

What Amartya did not speak about that night was that behind the joyous façade and sense of celebration, he was deeply saddened by the sudden death of his close friend and colleague Mahbub-ul-Haq who had passed away rather suddenly due to pneumonia. Amartya had come to Sweden directly from New York where he had attended the memorial service. At the service, Amartya had said with a heavy heart, "I shall miss my friend a lot and I am sure that if he had been alive he would have been very pleased to see me get the prize."

Immediately after that night, in Stockholm Amartya departed to visit the one person who would have wanted to attend the awards ceremony more than anybody else but could not—his mother. Back home in India, celebrations had already begun. On the long journey to Calcutta, Amartya realized he had turned into a celebrity overnight as he was often stopped and asked for autographs. The quiet academic was as yet unused to the recognition, but he would have to get used to it.

At London's Heathrow Airport, en route to Calcutta, he had a stroke of bad luck when one of his bags containing a replica of the Nobel Prize medal was stolen. It was not just Amartya or the airport officials but the entire country that heaved a collective sigh of relief when it was discovered it was only the replica and not the actual medal!

At Calcutta's Dum Dum airport, Amartya was received by the State Finance Minister Ashim Dasgupta and the Mayor Prasanta Chattopadhyay. Although he was honoured, he was eager to meet with his family, especially his sister Suparna Dutta who had recently lost her husband. He was able to spend only a little time with his sister and mother before leaving for the city of his childhood, Dhaka, Bangladesh, and attending numerous functions in Calcutta held in his honour.

Amartya's arrival in India after his win was nothing short of a celebration. He toured the country fulfilling numerous obligations, receiving honours and awards and meeting with various heads of state. In New Delhi, Amartya and his wife Emma Rothschild visited then Prime Minister A.B. Vajpayee, then Congress President Sonia Gandhi as well as then Finance Minister, Yashwant Sinha.

The West Bengal Government held a civic reception in honour of Amartya and used the function to make a public pledge to universalize primary education in the state by the year 2002. Finance Minister Asim Dasgupta announced that the project was also intended to bring down the infant mortality rate in West Bengal to 30 per 1,000. Dasgupta also announced the establishment of a research institute that would focus on issues of Sen's concern, such as land reform, primary education and health care.

Amartya spent much of this visit to India making public addresses at various universities. The most noteworthy of these was his address to the students of Delhi's Jawaharlal Nehru University (JNU). Reporting on this address, the newspaper *The Hindu* wrote, "Having attended scores of such occasions since being awarded the Nobel Prize, Sen confessed to a desire to depart from the usual pattern of convocation addresses. The subject of his address at JNU was stirring in its conception and delivery."

The most overwhelming part of being in India that month was the constant adulation Amartya received everywhere he went, whether it was at an official gathering or just walking down a street. Stations, airports and streets were constantly lined with people eager to see and meet India's favourite son. But nowhere was the reception warmer than in Santiniketan and Calcutta, the cities most closely associated with his childhood. *The Hindu* described his visit as follows: "Men, women and children gathered in large numbers at railway stations and airports to greet Sen; they lined the streets along which he drove and thronged public functions at which he spoke; they stood patiently outside the gates of his home in Santiniketan, waiting for a chance to see him and, if lucky, speak to him, get an autograph and shake his hand. They were celebrating the success of one of their own." Amartya was initially uncomfortable with the public adulation and displayed thorough humility in its acceptance.

The Visva-Bharati University where he had studied as a child felicitated Amartya at a quiet, dignified ceremony, similar to the one held for Tagore's felicitation after his win. Amartya was touched and awed when he discovered the ceremony was being held at the Amra Kunj or the mango grove where Rabindranath Tagore too had been felicitated after his Nobel

Prize win in 1913. Says *The Hindu,* "The early morning function at the Amra Kunj was marked by the elegance and gentle pace that are characteristic of that unusual campus. Sen, dressed in white dhoti and kurta with a yellow batik scarf around his neck, was brought to the stage by a procession of young children and members of the University. Vice-Chancellor Dilip Sinha presented Santiniketan's eminent son a 'manpatra', a letter of honour or felicitation, which was read out in Sanskrit and Bengali." At the ceremony, his close friend Sunil Sengupta put up a programme showing the similarities between Santiniketan's two favourite sons—Amartya Sen and Rabindranath Tagore. Later, the Bolpur Citizens' Committee organized a public meeting attended by cheering school children, eager to hear the Nobel Laureate.

The most touching incident however occurred one evening while Amartya was walking around the campus. Amartya tells of a man who came up to him and placed a pen in his hand. Thinking that the man wanted his autograph, Amartya asked, "Where is the book?" The man replied, "Sir, I don't want your autograph. If you can just touch the pen and bless it, I am sure my son will pass his exam."

For the remainder of the month, Amartya basked in the glory of his achievement and the attention being poured on him by his countrymen at one function or another. But even in the midst of his newfound fame, he made sure he spent time with his old friends, teachers and colleagues.

Santiniketan that month was a gaggle of voices from Amartya's past and present, each raised with stories and anecdotes of the accomplished professor. There were accolades from his teachers and humorous anecdotes from his friends. Dipankar

Chatterjee, a friend and classmate of Amartya, recalled, "Amartya would study hard at night and do other things during the day, so people would say he never worked but still did well!"

What emerged from all those voices was one consistent thread—that Amartya Sen's victory was no surprise or shock to those who had known him since his youngest days.

Death comes to all, but great achievements
raise a monument which shall endure
until the sun grows cold

— *George Fabricus* —

14

IMMORTALITY

After the Nobel Prize, Amartya Sen's life did not alter as dramatically as public perception of him did. The man whose brilliance thus far was known only in academic circles suddenly became a household name. Overnight, almost, he became a hero for every student in India, for every parent, for every teacher. The success he achieved, the work he put in to achieve it and the positive spirit he brought to every challenge life threw his way have all become an inspiration.

In these achievements, parallels have often been drawn between Amartya Sen and Rabindranath Tagore. On the surface, the similarities between the two are evident. Both

Sen and Tagore were the first Indians in their respective fields to receive the Nobel Prize (Tagore won the Nobel for Literature in 1913), both are Bengalis and, perhaps the strongest connection of all, Amartya was a student at Visva-Bharati in Santiniketan, the open-air school set up by Tagore. Sen's association with Tagore however goes farther back to the days his grandfather, Kshiti Mohan Sen, helped Tagore set up Santiniketan.

Although more of an academician than an artist, like Tagore, Amartya too is a lover of art, classical shows and plays. This he perhaps gets from his mother, Amita Sen, who performed many of Tagore's dance dramas. In this regard, Sen's close friend Sunil Sengupta recalls an incident when on a visit to London, Sengupta was given the choice to either attend a staged performance of *My Fair Lady* or attend a dinner hosted by Sen's wife, Emma. Helping the confused Sengupta, Amartya whispered into his ear, "There will be many Eva dinners. But don't miss the show."

On a more philosophical level as well, there are congruities between Sen and Tagore, many of which Sen realizes only today. In his words, "[Tagore] was clearly the strongest influence [in Santiniketan]. Later on, thinking about it, I thought that I agreed much more with Tagore than I recognized then, because his presence was so strong there. There wasn't enough contrast. But only when I was thinking about other people who influenced my thinking, like Mahatma Gandhi, John Stuart Mill, Karl Marx and Adam Smith, I did think that Tagore had a very particular role which I wasn't fully aware of at that time."

One of these influences on Sen was the multi-cultural,

'one world' attitude Tagore brought to Santiniketan and instilled in every student. Tagore was a firm believer in imbibing the products of the culture and traditions of countries all over the world. He believed that simply by virtue of enjoying something, it became part of your culture and personality, regardless of where it originated. This thinking perhaps emerged from the fact that Tagore's own family was a product of the Hindu, Mohammedan and British cultures, and the young Tagore was educated in Sanskrit as well as Arabic, Persian and Islamic traditions.

One of the greatest examples of Tagore's sense of tolerance and respect for other cultures can be seen in the fact that he is the only person in the world to have authored the national anthems of two countries—the *Jana Gana Mana* for the largely Hindu country of India and *Amar Sonar Bangla* (My Golden Bengal) for the largely Muslim nation of Bangladesh. In an article in *The New York Review*, Sen has expressed his delight at the fact that Tagore is the author of the national anthems of the two countries he calls home.

Sen's nomadic lifestyle and eagerness to chase knowledge no matter where in the world, travelling from campus to campus, is a clear indication that his beliefs too are along the same lines. Like Tagore, Sen has a deep love and admiration for Indian culture, but he is more than willing to step outside his country's boundaries to interact with other cultures and extract the best of them. This has perhaps been one of the greatest learnings Sen received at Santiniketan—a direct influence of Tagore's own attitudes.

Today, Sen is an admirer of Tagore and acknowledges the influence he had on him—not so much on the content of his work but more on the manner in which he went about it. Although they never met, Tagore's thinking, imparted to Sen through his teachers at Santiniketan, has clearly helped mould the way he thinks and feels about life and the world.

Sen's mother Amita put it best when she said, "Tagore is his *dhrubatara,* his guiding star, and Santiniketan is the place where he comes to seek peace."

Ever humble, Sen has often expressed that he can in no way be compared to a legend like Tagore. Perhaps in his humility he forgets that it was Tagore who gave him his name—a name that means 'immortal'. And there is no doubt that Amartya Sen will certainly remain forever immortal, a legend, an icon, an inspiration.